Also by Zen Master Seung Sahn

Dropping Ashes on the Buddha (1976)

Bone of Space: Zen Poems (1982)

Ten Gates: The Kong-an Teaching
of Zen Master Seung Sahn (1987)

The Whole World Is A Single Flower:
365 Kong-ans for Everyday Life (1992)

ONLY DON'T KNOW

The Teaching Letters
of Zen Master Seung Sahn

Primary Point Press
Cumberland, Rhode Island

Copyright ©1982 Providence Zen Center,
528 Pound Road, Cumberland, Rhode Island 02864

Second printing, 1985
Third printing, 1991
Fourth printing, 1992

Printed in the United States of America

Library of Congress Cataloging in Publication Data:

Seung, Sahn.
    Only don't know.

    1. Religious life (Zen Buddhism)   2. Priests, Zen —
United States — Correspondence.   3. Zen Buddhists —
United States — Correspondence.   I. Title
BQ9286.S45   1982   294.3'927   82-17380
ISBN 0-942795-03-2

Originally published by Four Seasons Foundation, San Francisco

Cover calligraphy of the character MU and Zen circle
by Mu Yoe Ko-sa

Primary Point Press logo by Grazyna Perl

Primary Point Press
528 Pound Road
Cumberland, Rhode Island 02864
(401) 658-1476
FAX (401) 658-1188

CONTENTS

A don't-know mind is a before-thinking mind.
Before thinking is clear like space.
Clear like space is clear like a mirror.

INTRODUCTION

Zen Master Seung Sahn is addressed and referred to by his students as Soen Sa Nim, a title meaning "Honored Zen Teacher." His letters are all signed "S.S.," the initials for Seung Sahn, Korean for "High Mountain." This is the name of the mountain on which Hui Neng, the sixth Zen patriarch, attained enlightenment, and it is the name Soen Sa Nim received when his teacher, Zen Master Ko Bong, gave him Transmission of the Dharma.

Soen Sa Nim is the first Korean Zen Master to teach in the West. He was born in 1927 of Christian parents at a time when Korea was under severely repressive Japanese military rule. At the age of seventeen he joined the underground Korean independence movement, was arrested by the Japanese, and narrowly escaped execution. Upon his release he and a few friends stole several thousand dollars from their parents to finance an abortive attempt to join the Free Korean Army across the Manchurian border.

After World War II, while studying Western philosophy at Dong Guk University, Soen Sa Nim became disenchanted with radical politics as a solution to social problems, and disillusioned with academic studies as a means to understand the truth. He shaved his head and went into the mountains, vowing not to return until he understood the meaning of life and death. It was at this time that he first encountered Buddhism. After a period of studying the sutras he took vows as a Buddhist monk in 1948, and shortly after being ordained he began an arduous one-hundred-day meditation retreat in the mountains. The enlightenment that he attained on this retreat was subsequently validated by three Zen Masters, and at the age of twenty-two he received Transmission of the Dharma, certification as a Zen Master in his own right, from Zen Master Ko Bong.

After practicing in silence for three years, Soen Sa Nim became active in the Chogye order, the major school of Buddhism in Korea. He was instrumental in the revitalization of the order and became abbot of five temples in Seoul. Later he spent nine years in Japan and founded temples in Tokyo and Hong Kong.

In 1972 Soen Sa Nim came to the United States and settled in Providence, Rhode Island. Soon after his arrival, a small group of undergraduates from Brown University became his students. Out of their practice the Providence Zen Center was formed, now head temple for some twenty other Zen Centers and affiliated groups in the United States and Canada, all founded by students practicing under Soen Sa Nim's direction. An organization called the Kwan Um School of Zen has been formed to support this network of centers. The list of centers extends world-wide, with groups in Europe, Korea, Brazil, and South Africa.

During his first decade in the West, Soen Sa Nim also taught by correspondence, personally answering every letter that was written to him. Unless the writer requested otherwise, each letter, together with Soen Sa Nim's reply, was placed in dossiers (containing over 2000 letters total) which were distributed to each of the Zen Centers. Formal practice at each of the Zen Centers includes the reading of a letter to Soen Sa Nim and his reply. The volume from which the letters are read is referred to as the kong-an book *(Japanese: koan)*, and indeed these letters, originating in a variety of private concerns, have become kong-ans: public documents recording the Zen

Master's teaching on a specific occasion and used for the instruction of Zen students at large.

The letters in Only Don't Know have been chosen from this collection. They have been arranged in eight categories that range from broad areas of human concern to the particulars of Zen practice. Correspondents include Zen Center residents, but also, more typically, other Zen students seeking advice about their lives and practice, and occasionally engaging in Dharma combat with their teacher.

These letters exemplify the importance of the teacher-student relationship in Zen training. Those who become students of a Zen Master usually do so because of a deep trust in his or her insight. Interchange with a teacher is a corner-stone of the Zen tradition; through dialogue, the Zen Master reflects the clarity of the student's mind. This collection is a sample of concerns of students during the course of their Zen practice. Beyond simple questions and answers, they convey the spirit of Zen training that comes alive in the relationship of a student to a Zen Master.

This book has six appendices. The first four contain traditional Zen teaching that Soen Sa Nim often refers to in his letters. The first, "Mind Meal," is a collection of ten important kong-ans Soen Sa Nim has chosen for his students to examine in depth during their practice with him. While he also uses hundreds of others, these ten lie at the heart of his kong-an teaching. The Temple Rules in Appendix II are Soen Sa Nim's selection of traditional Zen temple rules that he considers most useful and appropriate for day-to-day life at Zen Centers in the West. The Heart Sutra in Appendix III, a classic statement of Zen Buddhist teaching, is chanted in Zen monasteries throughout China, Korea, Japan, and now in the West. The Five Precepts are listed in Appendix IV. They are vows taken in a ceremony in which students formally become lay Buddhists and Soen Sa Nim's students. Appendix V is Soen

Sa Nim's "Zen Circle," a teaching device he uses to explain Zen practice. Appendix VI, the Glossary, translates and explains terms which may be unfamiliar to Western readers.

The title *Only Don't Know* echoes one of Soen Sa Nim's favorite expressions that goes to the heart of his teaching. The knowing that he enjoins against is the mind's enraptured production of its opinions, judgements, discriminations and preferences, creating the confusion in which most of us live and, in its wake, our own and other people's suffering. *Only Don't Know* means choosing to pay attention. When we choose to pay attention, this confusion is dispelled; just seeing, just hearing, or just perceiving the needs of others is the turning point for clarity and compassion.

The teaching that Soen Sa Nim offers us in this book was passed on to him by his teacher, Zen Master Ko Bong, and to Ko Bong by his teacher, Zen Master Mang Gong, in a lineage that can be traced back through the Korean Zen Masters, through the Chinese and Indian masters, and finally back to the Buddha himself. It is not new, but it is a unique expression of the Buddha's mind that is discovering itself now in the West.

Louise Sichel
Providence Zen Center

Stanley Lombardo
Kansas Zen Center

June, 1982

ACKNOWLEDGEMENTS

This book has been edited over the past three years by a number of Soen Sa Nim's students. From the Providence Zen Center, advisors on its teaching content were Master Dharma Teachers George Bowman and Barbara Rhodes. Jacob Perl began the editing process, and Merrie Fraser reviewed the selections and refined Soen Sa Nim's English. Sherry and Lawlor Rochester of the Ontario Zen Centre organized the letters and edited the material further. Becky Bernen of the Cambridge Zen Center researched the Glossary. Judy Roitman of the Kansas Zen Center and Carole Korzeniowsky of the Chogye International Zen Center of New York made suggestions on emphasis and organization.

The final editing was completed by Louise Sichel at the Providence Zen Center with the assistance of Zen Center Director Suzanne Bowman and Katrina Avery. The manuscript was typed by Zen Center Secretary Marcia Peters; Gillian Harrison corrected the proofs.

The experience of working together is not an unusual one for Soen Sa Nim's students. The opportunity to practice Zen by living and working together would not have been possible without the inspiration and example of our teacher, Zen Master Seung Sahn. In his letters and everyday life, he demonstrates with simplicity, generosity, humor and single-pointed energy that it is possible to give ourselves unselfishly, 100% to any situation. For this we all express our deepest gratitude.

Lincoln Rhodes, Abbot
Providence Zen Center

June, 1982

I. WHAT IS ZEN?

CORRECT MEDITATION

Berkeley, California
July 9, 1977

Dearest Soen Sa Nim,

Diana just called to tell me of your heart and diabetes problems.* I am so sorry you don't feel well. I am remembering what a shock it was when we first found out that my son had diabetes and would need to take insulin. He was only seventeen, and his pancreas worked irregularly, so the adjustment of his insulin dosage was dependent on his activity as well as on his food. But he soon learned to anticipate his needs and learned to drink orange juice when he overestimated. I am sure that by now you also have adjusted to your new treatment.

I was sorry to miss the last Big Sur Kido. Get well soon!

Love you,
Marge

July 15, 1977

Dear Marge,

Thank you for your letter. How are you?

I have just returned from the hospital. You worry about my body; thank you. Now I am following the hospital's instructions, and I am just beginning to take insulin. I had taken diabetes pills for fifteen years, but the doctor said that these pills damaged my heart, so I went to the hospital, took some heart

---

* In July of 1977, Soen Sa Nim went into the hospital to have his irregular heart beat monitored and to begin using insulin to control an advanced case of diabetes.

medicine, and now my heart is working correctly, so my body is no problem.

When I was in the hospital, many of the doctors there were interested in meditation. My doctors suggested that I try meditation so that my heart would get better quickly, so I did. When I first went to the hospital my heart was not beating in a regular way. This problem usually takes two or three months to fix. But I meditated, so it only took one week to fix, and the doctors were very surprised and happy. They said that now many doctors like meditation because it can help to fix your body. Several doctors wanted to learn more about meditation, so they arranged to come to my hospital room and I taught them a little about Zen.

I told them that "fixing-your-body" meditation is a kind of concentration yoga meditation, but it is not correct meditation. This kind of yoga meditation lets your body rest and become strong. Some yogis only sit in a quiet place, breathing in and breathing out, and sometimes they live for 100 years or 1,000 years. It is possible to keep your body this long, but eventually it will die.

Correct meditation means freedom from life and death. Our true self has no life and no death. I said that if you attain your true self, then if you die in one hour, in one day, or in one month, it is no problem. If you only do "fixing-your-body" meditation, your concern only will be with your body. But some day, when it's time for you to die, this meditation will not help you, so you will not believe in it. This means it is not correct meditation. If you do correct meditation, being sick sometimes is O.K.; suffering sometimes is O.K.; dying someday is O.K. The Buddha said, "If you keep a clear mind moment to moment, then you will get happiness everywhere."

How much do you believe in yourself? How much do you help other people? These are most important questions. Correct meditation helps you find your true way.

I told them that I had asked the man in the bed next to me, "What is the purpose of your life?" He had a good job, a good family, a good wife, but these things could not help him. So he said, "Nothing." He understood "nothing," but his understanding could not help him, so he was suffering. Zen means to attain this nothing-mind.

How do you attain nothing-mind? First you must ask, "What am I? What is the purpose of my life?" If you answer with words, this is only thinking. Maybe you say, "I am a doctor." But if you are with a patient and you are thinking, "I am a great doctor," you cannot perceive your patient's situation—you are caught in your thinking. Thinking is only understanding; like the man in the hospital you will find that understanding cannot help you. Then what? If you don't know, you must go straight—don't know.

Don't-know mind cuts through thinking. It is before thinking. Before thinking there is no doctor, no patient; also no God, no Buddha, no "I", no words—nothing at all. Then you and the universe become one. We call this nothing-mind, or primary point. Some people say this is God, or universal energy, or bliss, or extinction. But these are only teaching words. Nothing-mind is before words.

Zen is attaining nothing-mind, and using nothing-mind. How can you use it? Make nothing-mind into big-love-mind. Nothing means no I-my-me, no hindrance, so this mind can change to action-for-all-people mind. This is possible. Nothing-mind neither appears nor disappears. If you do correct meditation, nothing-mind becomes strong and you perceive your situation clearly: what you see, hear, smell, taste, and touch are the truth, without thinking. So your mind is like a mirror. Then moment to moment you can keep your correct situation. When a doctor is with his patients, if he drops I-my-me and becomes one with them, then helping them is possible. When a doctor goes home and he is with his family, if he keeps 100%

his father's mind, then understanding what is best for them is clear. Just like this. The blue mountain does not move. The white clouds float back and forth.

So, the doctors liked Zen. Maybe they will try practicing!

I hope you only go straight—don't know, attain nothing-mind, use nothing-mind, and save all beings from suffering.

> Yours in the Dharma,
> S. S.

LETTERS FROM JAIL

> Atlanta, Georgia
> June 8, 1978

Dear Sir:

One of your students suggested that I write directly to you and that you would be kind enough to offer some advice.

I am incarcerated at Atlanta Penitentiary and would like to have a suggestion on how to practice Zen while I am in prison.

I have already read many books on Zen, including the essays by D. T. Suzuki.

Sometimes when I feel as though I have achieved satori, I seem to lose it and fall back to my old self again. Why am I unable to maintain my gains in the area of Zen?

Thank you.

> Sincerely,
> Robert

> June 20, 1978

Dear Robert,

Thank you for your letter. How are you? It is wonderful that you wrote to me directly.

In your letter you said you are in jail. That is a wonderful Zen Center! I also have been in jail.* Maybe that jail made me become a Zen Master. Maybe jail will make you become a Zen Master!

You said you have read many books on Zen. Not good, not bad. If you have your direction, then all Zen books, the Bible, and all the Sutras will help you find your true way. But if you have no direction and you read many books about Zen then your mind will be filled with thinking.

What is your correct direction? Do you have one? You must show me! If you don't understand, throw away books! I ask you, what are you? Where are you coming from? What is your name? How old are you? When you die, where will you go? These are all simple questions. Maybe you say, "My name is Robert." That is your body's name. What is your true self's name? Maybe you say, "I am 35 years old." But that is your body's age. What is your true age? Tell me, tell me! If you don't understand, only go straight—don't know. Don't check your feelings; don't check your mind; don't check your understanding.

Next, you sometimes feel that you have experienced satori. This is *feeling* satori; when this feeling disappears, satori disappears, so it is not correct satori. True satori is unmoving, unchanging; it has no feeling, no thought. It is no satori. The Heart Sutra says, "No attainment, with nothing to attain." You must attain that.

I often talk about primary point. What is primary point? If you have a scale with nothing on it, the indicator points to zero. When you put something on the scale, the pointer swings to read the weight. When you remove the weight, the pointer returns to zero. This is primary point. After you find your primary point, then good feelings may come or bad feelings may come, so your pointer swings in one direction or

---

* Seung Sahn Soen-Sa's prison experience is recounted in *Dropping Ashes on the Buddha.*

the other, but this doesn't matter. When the feeling is over, the pointer will swing back to zero.

But if you haven't found your primary point, then it is like taking a heavy object off the scale with the pointer still indicating 10 pounds, or only returning part of the way back towards zero. Then you have a problem. Your scale does not weigh accurately. If you put another heavy object on it, it might break completely.

So first you must find your primary point. Then you must keep it strong. A taxi has weak shock absorbers, so it bounces up and down when it hits a small bump. A train has strong shock absorbers, so it is very steady. If you keep your primary point, your mind-spring will become stronger and stronger. A big problem will come and your mind will move, but it will soon return to primary point. Finally your mind will be very strong, and it will be able to carry any load. Then saving all beings from suffering is possible.

Zen is not special. If you make something, if you make "special"—then you have something; you have "special." But this something, this "special" cannot help you. Put it all down. What are you doing now? When you are doing something, you must *do* it. Then you are already complete. Then you will find your primary point. Then you will understand your correct situation and your correct job. To do this you must only go straight. Don't know. It doesn't matter if you are in jail or out of jail; already you will have freedom from life and death.

Here is a kong-an for your homework:

Hyang Eom's Up a Tree ("Mind Meal," Fifth Gate)

Master Hyang Eom said, "It is like a man up a tree who is hanging from a branch by his teeth; his hands cannot grasp a bough, his feet cannot touch the tree; he is tied and bound. Another man under the tree asks him, 'Why did Bodhidharma come to China?' If he does not answer, he evades his duty and he will be killed. If he answers, he will lose his life. If you are in the tree, how do you stay alive?"

I hope you only go straight—don't know, soon find your primary point, finish your homework, and save all beings from suffering.

Yours in the Dharma,
S. S.

Atlanta, Georgia
July 10, 1978

Zen Master Seung Sahn,

Thank you so much for your letter. It was very nice to hear from you and to receive your advice.

I am most puzzled by your statements regarding satori. Isn't it true that the goal of Zen is to achieve satori, a state of intuitive awareness? You say that true satori "is unmoving, is unchanging; it has no feeling, no thought." These are all negative expressions of satori. What is it in the positive sense? Is it not a state of total happiness, a whole and complete mind?

You say there is nothing to attain. Please explain this to me in terms of satori. How do I reach a state of satori? How will I know when I am in a state of satori?

I am awaiting your response to my previous letter. I am sure that you are very busy, but I wonder if you could make recommendations on how I can advance my Zen training while I am yet in prison?

There is a great deal of noise in prison and I am having difficulty concentrating during sitting while in my cell. Furthermore, I am not sure of what I should be doing while concentrating during the time I sit Zen. Can you advise me on how to go about meditating properly and what goals, if any, I should keep in mind?

Yours in the Dharma,
Robert

Dear Robert,

Thank you for your letter. My reply is a little late because I have just finished Cambridge Zen Center's Yong Maeng Jong Jin and we have just returned to the Providence Zen Center. In your letter you say that you want satori. If you want satori, satori is far, far away. If you don't want satori, you can see, you can hear, you can smell—everything is satori. So put down "I want something." If you keep I-my-me mind and try sitting Zen, you will not get satori for infinite time. If you make your I-my-me mind disappear, then you already have satori. O.K.?

In your letter, you also said it is noisy in your prison cell so you have a problem when you meditate. If your mind is noisy, even if you go to a mountaintop, it is noisy. If your mind is not noisy, even if you are in a factory, it is very quiet. How you keep your just-now mind is very important. You check inside, and you check outside—checking, checking, checking—so you have many questions. Put it all down. Then the whole universe is very quiet.

"All formations are appearing and disappearing. That is the law of appearing and disappearing. If you make appearing and disappearing disappear, that stillness is bliss." (Mahaparinirvana Sutra)

You asked for recommendations on how to advance your Zen training while in prison, and what goals to keep in mind. "I want to try something. I want something. I want to get something." If you make this "I" disappear, then "I want to try something, I want something, and I want to get something" will all disappear: already you are complete. Where does this "I" come from? An eminent teacher said, "Without thinking, just like this is truth." Descartes said, "I think; therefore, I am." If you are not thinking, what?

Being in prison is sometimes very difficult. But, if you make your opinion, your condition, and your situation disappear, then a difficult situation is O.K.; noise is O.K.; your mind will be unmoving. So, when you are doing something, you must do it! That is Zen. I hope you only go straight—don't know, make I-my-me disappear, attain Enlightenment, and save all beings from suffering.

Yours in the Dharma,
S. S.

HOW DO I EXPLAIN ZEN
PRACTICE TO OTHER PEOPLE?

Cambridge, Massachusetts
March 17, 1978

Dear Soen Sa Nim,

Thank you very much for your letter.

I've been having difficulty explaining Zen and my practice to my family and friends, especially my parents. Most of them like the questions, "What is life? What is death? What is our correct job in life?" They say they have asked these questions themselves but feel that we can never know the answers: "Only God knows."

Another thing many people say to me is that it is impossible to save all people from suffering. They feel that life is suffering and that we cannot change that. Also, they cannot understand how sitting Zen or chanting or bowing can help other people. It seems self-centered and selfish to them to be always "thinking about yourself" and "doing nothing" in a Zen Center away from other people. They feel that a person should be "out in the world" working with people who need help.

I would like to ask you what a good answer would be to these questions.

Thank you very much for your teaching.

Sincerely yours,
Steve

March 22, 1978

Dear Steve,

Thank you for your beautiful letter. How are you?

In your letter you asked about the questions of saving all people from suffering and what life and death are. These questions are very easy.

Your friends and family have ideas about many things; they hold onto them but don't understand that they are attached to them. Originally there is nothing. If you make something, you have something. If you don't make anything, then already you are complete.

What is death? What is life? Our bodies have life and death, but our true selves have no life and no death. They don't understand their true selves, so they have life and death. They say, "Only God knows." What is God? Do they know God? How do they know that only God knows?

If you wish to understand God, then you must first understand your true self. This is the first course.

How do you understand your true self? What are you? Do you know? If you don't know, only go straight—don't know. Then this don't-know mind cuts off all thinking, and your only-me situation, only-me condition, and only-me opinion disappear. Then your correct situation, correct condition, and correct opinion appear—very simple. An eminent teacher said, "You can understand for yourself whether water is hot or cold." Understanding your true self is not special.

Next course: if you are thinking, then your mind and my mind are different. If you cut off all thinking, then your mind, my mind, all people's minds are not different. An eminent teacher said, "One is many; many are one." So if you cut off all thinking there is no I-my-me. Then you can *keep* your correct situation, correct condition and correct opinion from moment to moment. This is already world peace; you have already saved all people.

So first: how do you cut off all thinking? Already I asked you, "What are you?" If you don't know, only go straight— don't know.

Next: how do you keep don't-know mind moment to moment? You must try, try, try. So every day at a Zen Center we bow, chant, sit, and work together. Sometimes we do Yong Maeng Jong Jin; sometimes we do a Kido. These actions help us practice moment to moment: what are you doing now? If your mind is not clear, don't keep your ideas; only don't know. Slowly your desire-thinking, your anger-thinking, your ignorance-thinking disappear, so your don't-know mind grows strong and becomes clear.

Therefore, when you sit, just sit. When you chant, just chant. When you bow, just bow. That is most important. If you practice this way, then when you teach other people, just teach. Only teach; only help them. Don't worry whether or not they understand; only try. If you are trying 100%, then your teaching is complete and your mind-light will shine to them. Some day they will understand this.

So don't worry—just try. Trying is better than a Zen Master, better than Buddha, better than God. It is already Great Love, Great Compassion, and the Great Bodhisattva Way. Don't check your feelings; don't check your mind; don't check your understanding; don't check outside. Then there is no inside, no outside, no I, no you, no they: you are one with your situation. That is very important.

I hope you only go straight—don't know, keep a mind which is clear like space, attain Enlightenment, and save all beings from suffering.

Yours in the Dharma,
S. S.

FIND YOUR CENTER,
LIKE A DHARMA TOY

Berkeley, California

October 21, 1977

Dear Soen Sa Nim,

I hope you are well. Thank you for the good Kido. I got lots of energy from it. I have been doing Kwan Seum Bosal. I try to do it whenever I'm not doing anything else with my mind. But still, there is a lot of small I, many thoughts. All this thinking makes me unhappy. So, when I went to see Diana, I said, "I am depressed." So, for an hour, we did therapy. Then, at the end of the hour, Diana said, "Do more Kwan Seum Bosal, and come stay at the Zen Center." So, I am going to move into the Zen Center as soon as I can find someone to sublet my place. I am sure this together action will be very good for me.

Love,

Maggie

November 7, 1977

Dear Maggie,

Thank you for your letter. How are you and the Berkeley Empty Gate Zen Center family? I'm glad you liked the Kido.

You say you are doing Kwan Seum Bosal whenever you are not doing anything else with your mind. This is not good, not bad. I ask you: where is your center? That is most important. If you don't lose your center, then any action is no problem. Also, how strong is your center? I tell you, when you are doing something, do it. When you are doing something 100%, this is your center; this is clear mind. But be very careful. If you keep your ideas, your condition, your situation, you will lose your center to any action you are doing.

I often talk about lost mind, one mind, and clear mind. Suppose a man and a woman are having sex. They have lost their minds and are very, very happy. Just then, a robber breaks in with a gun and says, "Give me your money!" All their happiness disappears, and they are very scared. "Oh, help me, help me!" This is small mind. It is constantly changing, as outside conditions change. We also call this lost mind.

Next, someone is doing mantra. His mind is not moving at all. There is no inside or outside, only true emptiness. The robber appears, "Give me money!" But this person is not afraid. Only *"Om mani padme hum, om mani padme hum."* "Give me money, or I'll kill you!" He doesn't care. Already, there is no life and no death, so he is not in the least afraid. This is one mind.

Next is clear mind. A person keeping don't-know mind is walking down the street. The robber appears. "Give me your money!" This person tests his mind: "How much do you want?" "Give me everything!" This robber is very strong; nothing will stop him. "O.K.," and he gives the robber all his money. He is not afraid, but his mind is very sad. He is thinking, "Why are you doing this? Now, you are winning, but in the future, you will have much suffering." The robber looks at him and sees that he is not afraid, and that there is only strong compassion on his face. So, the robber is a little confused. The person is already teaching him the correct way, and maybe some day he will remember and be able to understand.

Keeping clear mind comes from having a strong center. In the Orient, there is a toy called a Dharma Toy, named after Bodhidharma. It's a little figure with a rounded, weighted bottom that rocks when it is tapped. Even if you turn it completely upside down, it returns again to its correct position by itself, because the toy has a center. If you are keeping Kwan Seum Bosal strongly, then when someone talks to you, then only talk. But when they leave, you can soon return to Kwan Seum Bosal. If, at that time, you hold something in your mind, you cannot return to Kwan Seum Bosal. So don't hold anything. The name for that is clear mind, Kwan Seum Bosal, don't-know, your center. So don't worry. Only go straight— Kwan Seum Bosal.

You are moving into the Berkeley Empty Gate Zen Center— that's wonderful news. Practicing and living with other Zen students is the number-one way to help your center become strong.

I hope you only go straight—Kwan Seum Bosal, find your Dharma center, get Enlightenment, and save all beings from suffering.

Yours in the Dharma,
S. S.

YOU MUST LEARN FROM YOUR DAUGHTER

Ile Ife, Nigeria
October 5, 1977

Dear Keen-Eyed Venerable Teacher of Hard Training,

I take refuge in the three Jewels.

Allow me to greet you from the land of ebon majesty.

In 1975, I was present at a Dharma Talk you gave at the Arica Institute in Boston. Very recently, I obtained a copy of *Dropping Ashes on the Buddha*, and I have enjoyed reading it very much indeed. Also my one-year-old daughter Tara has very much enjoyed eating the cover. So, my question to you now is, "How do you teach a one-year-old brown Tara not to eat the Buddha?"

It is a very heavy rainy season now, and this morning, on my drive to work, I saw the "Federal Public Enlightenment" vehicle parked by the side of the road, while the driver relieved himself in the bush.

An incense ash falls
Immense thunder.
No sky is bluer.
A golden rooster cannot
Stand on one leg
And chase butterflies
While a Dharma-cat
Pisses on the ape
Who drops ashes on the Buddha.

I hope you find the time to write me.

Sincerely,
Harvey

November 6, 1977

Dear Wonderful Dharma Friend, Harvey,

How are you and your Buddha-eating baby? Thank you for your letter. You are very far away, but you are very close.

In your letter, you said you came to the Dharma talk at Arica Institute in 1975. That is wonderful. You made this good karma, so now you and I become very close.

You said that you read *Dropping Ashes on the Buddha*. That is very good. You also said that your daughter ate the cover, and you asked me how to teach a one-year-old brown Tara not to eat the Buddha. Your daughter is better than you because she can eat Buddha, but you cannot. Your daughter is stronger than Buddha, so she eats Buddha. Already she has graduated.

Eating Buddha means no Buddha. Long ago someone asked Zen Master Ma Jo, "What is Buddha?" He answered, "Mind is Buddha; Buddha is mind." The next day, another person asked the same question and Ma Jo said, "No mind, no Buddha." What is true Buddha? If you eat Buddha, then Buddha has no name, no form, no speech, and no words. Name-Buddha and form-Buddha both disappear. So you must learn from your daughter, and eat all the Buddhas of the past, the present, and the future. You ask, "How can I teach my daughter?" This is a big mistake. You must learn from your daughter!

Dropping Ashes on the Buddha is all bad speech, so your daughter is teaching you, "Don't read *Dropping Ashes on the Buddha*. That is the true way!" Your daughter understands my teaching. My teaching is only to put it all down. Only go straight—don't know. Maybe you are very attached to words, so your daughter ate *Dropping Ashes on the Buddha*. So Tara's answer is very good. It is better than yours.

Your story about the "Federal Public Enlightenment" vehicle is very interesting. There are 84,000 kinds of Enlightenment. But, if you add the Federal Public Enlightenment, you get 84,001. Maybe you like this last Enlightenment.

Your poem is wonderful. You say, "No sky is bluer." These are very interesting words. I say, "No sky is no earth." Then, how can you stay alive? Maybe, you become bluer. Then, you can live. Then, how can you become bluer? That is a very important point!

I hope you only go straight—don't know, eat all the Buddhas of the past, present, and future, attain Enlightenment, and save all beings from suffering.

Yours in the Dharma,
S. S.

ZEN IS EVERYDAY MIND

Wiscasset, Maine
June 29, 1978

Dear Soen Sa Nim,

I'm on vacation, away from my writing, with my wife and son. Yesterday, while at the beach, we noticed a man meditating. He was sitting in formal Zen-like posture, upright, by the edge of the sea, in the midst of the beach crowd. It first struck me as ostentatious to sit so publicly. Then the sitter got up and walked without hesitation into the icy sea-water—water that was so cold only a few of the others at the beach could get into it at all, and then only with great struggle. No one stayed in for more than a few seconds, except for the man who had been sitting. He remained there, floating about, for fifteen or twenty minutes.

My question is this: Was that true emptiness—being able to walk into the ice-cold water, apparently feeling nothing? That water was *cold* as far as I was concerned. But should I as a Zen student expect to attain something like that ability? Even though there is nothing to attain? What is true emptiness? Something special? Or the clarity of moment-to-moment practice?

Zen practice for me remains steady. Trying to keep clear all the time, failing, thinking, and sometimes not thinking. I still haven't found the Zen penpoint that will help my writing. Perhaps I'm writing with it now, but I don't *know* it yet, in my bones. So my search, and my not knowing, continue.

The April Yong Maeng Jong Jin at Cambridge with Master Dharma Teacher George Bowman was very fine. You were right. He is a wonderful teacher with much of your own simple, direct, no-bullshit style. I plan to attend the July Yong Maeng Jong Jin at Cambridge and will hope to see you then. Thank you very much for your earlier letter. It has helped me a lot.

> I am still sitting. Why?
> Katz!
> Sunlight on the forest floor. Gold stripes on a bed of pine
>   needles.

Here is a beach-poem for you:

> Waves that talk for hours to the beach
>   say nothing.

Wind that moves tree boughs back and forth
   does nothing.
Sunlight gilds the world without a sound.
   and still the world is never silent.
In all this vast space,
   empty sea, sand, and sky for miles and miles.
only I am confused,
walking the beach for hours,
foolishly searching,
looking for truth (or something),
missing, in front of me,
the shells, the sand,
the sound of waves.

Tom

July 6, 1978

Dear Tom,

Thank you very much for your letter. How are you and your family?

You had a vacation and went to the ocean with your family. That is wonderful. You said that on the beach, you saw a man sitting in a very formal meditation posture, and then he got up and went into the icy sea-water, where he stayed for fifteen or twenty minutes. Then you asked if this was true emptiness, and if a Zen student should expect to attain something like that ability. If inside you have I-my-me, this is called "*yeo hung shim*," which means "hero-mind." In Buddhism, there is a difficult kind of practice called Tantra practice. People who do this try a lot of mantra practice, then become one mind; then they break ice and go into the water for ten or twenty minutes or go into a fire for ten or twenty minutes. Or, after they try mantra and become one mind, they bathe in hot or boiling oil or sit on a bed of nails. These are all tests of perseverance-

mind. Then, if they master these practices, they go on to the next higher class of Tantra. After they have finished all of these practices, they get magic powers. That is called Tantra practice. This is not Zen, O.K.?

Zen is clear mind, always clear mind. Clear mind means that everyday mind is truth. Cold water is cold; hot water is hot—not special. If somebody thinks, "I want to experience difficult practicing," then O.K. But if they always keep a difficult practice, that is making something. If you make something, if you are attached to something, then that thing hinders you, and you cannot get complete freedom. *Maybe* you will get freedom from some things, but not perfectly complete freedom. Then what is perfectly complete? Don't hold I-my-me. Then you see; then you hear—everything is perfectly complete, not special.

Next, you said you cannot find your Zen penpoint. Not bad. If you find your penpoint, I will hit you thirty times. If you make Zen penpoint, then you have already lost your penpoint. Don't make Zen penpoint. Then you already have it, O.K.?

You did Yong Maeng Jong Jin with George. That is wonderful. George is a great teacher. Everybody likes him. You said you will do July Yong Maeng Jong Jin at Cambridge. That is also wonderful.

You also said, "I am still sitting. Why?
   Katz!
   Sunlight on the forest floor. Gold stripes
    on a bed of pine needles."

Not bad. These words are only "like-this." If you say, "I am still sitting," this means one point. "I" already has subject and object. If you had said "Buddha," or "Mind," or "Dharma," then your answer would have been wonderful; for this, only "like-this" is O.K. But for a one-point question, a one-point answer is needed. What is the just-like-this point of "I am sitting"?

Your poem is wonderful. Here is a poem for you:

Originally nothing. But waves always talk
to each other.
Originally emptiness. Always, wind and trees
are wrestling.
Sunlight is without color. But all things make
the colors they like.
Very, very quiet.

Somebody has eyes, so is confused.
If you have no eyes, then vast space, blue sea,
white sand, ten miles of no clouds, ten miles of clear sky.
Sun is setting in the West.
Shell's shadow grows longer and longer.

Yours in the Dharma,
S. S.

II. ON WORK

A SMALL NOISY ROOM WITH NO WINDOWS

Los Angeles, California
May 3, 1977

Dear Soen Sa Nim,

Three days ago I started a new job. I work with three women in a small room with no windows. Usually there is no work for more than two of the four of us. All day long they talk: they talk about sex, desires, angers. All day long the radio plays loud music about love and suffering.

What am I? I don't know. Still, what is reflected action? Am I to suffer every day, or can I reflect without "becoming"? Often, I find the atmosphere, the "way it is" there, depressing. My Bodhisattva mind keeps getting lost in fear and anger. The money is useful right now, but I fear becoming suffering.

O.K. I have a lot of pride. Some friends of mine are now making a lot of money. Often I think, "What do I do in this life?" I feel I waste myself at jobs like this one. Buddhist practice has almost literally saved my life. I know the thoughts and feelings I experience are not my true self but are just coming and going, coming and going. Still, blue is blue, fear is fear, desire is desire.

What should I do in this situation?

Thank you,
Michael

May 13, 1977

Dear Michael,

Thank you for your wonderful letter. How are you?

You say, "No windows . . . working with three women . . . all day long they talk of sex, desire and anger." This situation is your best teacher. It is better than a Zen Master, better than the Sutras, better than the Bible. If you hold onto the actions of these women, then you will become a demon. But if you don't hold on to their actions by judging or giving in to them their moment-to-moment actions will make you wise.

An eminent teacher said, "Wisdom is ignorance; ignorance is wisdom." This means, how do you keep a just-now mind? Checking your mind is ignorance. If you don't check your mind, then you can see, you can hear, you can smell—all things, just like this, are the truth. Then not only sex, desire, and anger, but also a dog barking, a chicken crowing—everything is the correct Dharma.

For example, when you go to the theater to see a comedy, your mind is laughing. When the picture is sad, your mind is sad. At that time, if you don't check your mind, then your mind does not move. Then funny is just funny, sad is sad, good is good, bad is bad. Everything appears clearly. That is correct wisdom. If you can find correct wisdom, your mind will already be clear like space. Then, moment to moment, reflected action is possible.

The whole world is like a theater. If you don't check your mind and don't check your feelings, then everything is the Sutras and the Bible. A small room with no windows is O.K. Talking about sex, desire, and anger is O.K. You will only ask, "How can I help them?" This is reflected action; this is the action of a Bodhisattva who always has great love and great sadness for all beings.

I hope that you put it all down and don't check anything. Only go straight—don't know. Then your don't-know mind will become clear, and in any situation reflected action is then possible. Then you can finish the Great Work of life and death and save all people from suffering.

Yours in the Dharma,
S. S.

MEMORIES OF VIETNAM

Hartford, Connecticut
May 29, 1979

Dear Soen Sa Nim,

I have recently renewed my efforts to sit Zen in the manner taught by you and Kapleau Roshi in Rochester, New York. However, now, as in the past, a problem faces me and diverts my attention to the point of giving up.

The problem I hope you—once a soldier yourself*—will help me overcome deals with my service in Vietnam. I was sent there twice. The first time was in 1968 and at that time I fought. Many died around me including children at an orphanage caught in a fierce cross-fire. The second time I was a medic with the marines and worked on the wounded. These events weigh heavily on my heart and mind and as such hamper my efforts when I sit Zen.

I will, if need be, contact the New Haven Zen Center for further advice.

Respectfully,
Paul

June 12, 1979

Dear Paul,

Thank you for your letter. How are you?

In your letter you talk about your service in Vietnam as a soldier and medic, seeing many people, including children, die around you, and treating the wounded. You say these things

---

* Soen Sa Nim served as a captain in the Korean Army.

weigh heavily on your heart and mind. You have already seen many dead people. Some day your body will also disappear—maybe tomorrow, maybe the day after tomorrow. Not only your body, but maybe this world will disappear tomorrow. All the large countries in the world have atom bombs. Maybe someday one person will make a mistake, push a button, set off all the missiles, and in a second the whole world will be destroyed. You saw many people die in the Vietnam war, so you have a strong feeling. But if your mind opens and you see this world, you will see that moment to moment there is great danger and you will be very unhappy, not knowing which way to turn.

A long time ago, Shakyamuni Buddha was a prince, soon to become a king. He had everything, but he wasn't satisfied, so he put it all down, cut his hair, went to the mountains, and sat under the Bodhi tree. One day he saw the morning star and got Enlightenment: he understood that your true self has no life and no death. You must understand that. Then, no problem. What are you? If you don't know, only go straight—don't know. World peace comes from this. So you must try, try, try. Then your experiences in Viet Nam will be your greatest teacher and will save all beings from suffering.

I hope you only go straight—don't know, which is clear like space, soon finish the great work of life and death, get Enlightenment, and save all beings from suffering.

Yours in the Dharma,
S. S.

SCIENCE AND ZEN

Berkeley, California
December 28, 1977

Dear Soen Sa Nim,

How are you? It was very nice to finally meet you at the Berkeley Empty Gate Zen Center during the December Yong Maeng Jong Jin.

During my interview at Yong Maeng Jong Jin last week, I asked you about the conflicts between scientific study and Zen practice. You answered that non-attachment to thinking is the key, and I understand that. But I would like to talk about the problem a bit more, because I think a reconciliation of the two would be marvelous, and because, for me, sometimes it seems hard to do scientific research without being attached—research can be most extraordinarily seductive.

Scientists, as I see it, try to build a view of the universe based on consistent, repeatable, communicable experience. The view is necessarily conceptual. It is also thoroughly imbued with the idea of physical causation, but primary causes must always be assumed and are often highy abstract. Maybe there's not much problem when one is dealing with very "external" problems such as the nature of a chemical compound or a physiological response, but what if one is investigating questions that point directly at the self, such as the biological evolution of human beings or the nature of consciousness? How does one reconcile the highly conceptual world-view of the scientist with the Zen View? I know one has to be careful not to confuse concepts with the experience to which they apply (sort of like maps and territories), but at the same time, the concepts are part of the experience. How can this be resolved? Maybe the only answer for me is to hurry up and try to get Enlightened.

What do you say?

I look forward to meeting you again in January. Take care.

Sincerely,
Eric

January 29, 1979

Dear Eric,

Thank you for your letter. How are you?

When I read your letter, I thought it was very interesting.

When I was in high school, I studied technical science, and I also had *many* questions. I thought about how this universe is made up of 115 elements. Where do the 115 elements come from? This was a big question for me, so I asked my teacher. My teacher said all elements come from "*mu guk*," which means nothingness. Then I did more thinking. If they are from true nothingness, how do these elements appear? My teacher gave me an example: sunlight has no color until it touches a drop of water, and then it makes a rainow. If one hundred people see this rainbow, then there are one hundred rainbows, but if nobody is there, then there is no rainbow. When you see a rainbow, you have a rainbow. I understood this. Then my teacher brought a machine to class that had a wheel made up of many colors. When the wheel spun around, there was no color, but when it stopped, there were many colors. So I thought, "Form is emptiness; emptiness is form."

All things in the universe are like this. They arise from emptiness and return to emptiness. So while low-class scientists only understand $1 + 2 = 3$, middle-class scientists understand that $1 + 2 = 0$. In other words, they understand that form is emptiness, and emptiness is form.

But high-class scientists ask, "Who makes 1, 2, 3, and 0? Who makes form and emptiness?" Both form and emptiness are concepts. Concepts are made by our own thinking. Descartes said, "I think; therefore I am." But if you are not thinking, then what? Before thinking there is no you, no I, no form, no emptiness. So even to say, "no form, no emptiness," is wrong. In true emptiness, before thinking, all things are just as they are. Form is form; emptiness is emptiness.

We have consciousness, and this consciousness is like a computer. A computer does not work by itself; somebody controls the computer. Our consciousness also does not make itself work; "something" controls our consciousness. Then our consciousness makes science. So this "something" controls consciousness, and consequently science. This "something" is not science, not consciousness, but has consciousness and science. So I say to you, if you attain "something," you understand consciousness and understand science. The name for that is Zen.

So, I ask you: What is "something?" And another question: $1 + 2 = 3$; $1 + 2 = 0$—which one is correct? Maybe you hit the floor. Then I say to you, "You understand one, but you don't understand two." What can you do? If you understand, you are a high-class scientist and Zen student, and they are not different. If you don't understand, only go straight—don't know. Many words are not necessary. Don't check your understanding. Don't make consciousness. Don't make science.

I hope you don't make anything, attain correct consciousness and correct science, soon finish the great work of life and death, get Enlightenment, and save all beings from suffering.

Yours in the Dharma,
S. S.

YOUR ORIGINAL JOB

Dear Soen Sa Nim,

How are you? It was good to see you again recently. We are all doing well. I think our recent Yong Maeng Jong Jin was very strong and people are once again pulling together and accepting responsibility as before. I think maybe our group of people at the Zen Center is very strong-willed and this causes all of us some problems, but I also think that we will be better able to deal with those problems as we get stronger together.

Soen Sa Nim, there is something that has occupied a lot of my thinking-mind energy over the past few years that I would like to share with you. For about the last seven or eight years I have had some doubts about whether I've chosen the right occupation. This has nothing to do with my economic well-being or any other success standards of our culture. By all those standards, I'm very well known, respected, rewarded, etc. But I've found it hard to believe in what I'm doing 100%. This has actually been made even clearer by regular practicing over the past four years. I haven't been able to really consider alternatives for the past few years because I've been sending my wife through school, but she will be finished in another year or so.

Years ago I seemed to have strong karma for both music and the medical profession; I chose music, but now I have big doubts. I'm attempting not to get attached to my condition and situation, but it seems that in order to keep Zen mind moment to moment, you have to believe in your actions 100% all of the time. This is difficult if I have fundamental doubts about the music that I'm writing down and about whether I should even be doing it.

Suzuki Roshi said once that people should be content to move a rock and not worry about catching the tail of a comet. I think I understand this teaching, and I know that American karma is to examine ourselves constantly and switch directions looking for *meaning!* But I don't think I'm on that trip. All I want to do is to become a good clear Dharma Teacher and find a moment-to-moment activity that I can become at one mind with, and (I hope) to help save all people.

If I were to consider going back to school in the next couple of years, it would put a big burden on my wife in terms of economics and lack of time together. My wife is willing and very supportive, but I wonder if it would be really fair. I realize that I have to work out and understand my own karma, and if I continue to practice I'll see these issues more clearly day by day. I wanted to write to you both because I haven't mentioned these matters to anyone and writing them down helps clarify one's mind, and also because if you have any teaching that is helpful I would, of course, be happy to receive it.

See you soon. Thanks for your time and teaching.

Yours in the Dharma,
John

March 30, 1977

Dear John,

How are you and your wife? You say YMJJ was strong and everyone is taking responsibility again. That is wonderful.

You asked me about your job. Before I have asked you: What is most important? Practicing every day. If you practice every day, then any kind of job is no problem.

When I was in Korea, a famous carpenter was my student. He was famous, but he did not like his job 100%. So one day when he visited me, he said, "My job is not good, not bad. Many people like my work. Sometimes I like it, but sometimes I don't like it. Sometimes I want to change my job." So he asked me, "What shall I do? Please teach me."

I asked him, "What is your original job?"

Then he said, "I am a carpenter."

So I said, "Carpentry is your body's job. What is your *true* job?"

"True job? What does this mean?"

"Your *mind* job," I said.

He said, "Mind job? My mind job is to keep Kwan Seum Bosal."

I said, "Do you *know* Kwan Seum Bosal?"

He said, "Don't know."

"You say, 'Don't know.' You have a question—what *is* Kwan Seum Bosal? So only go straight—Kwan Seum Bosal, and keep this question. This is your correct job.

"If you keep this original job, then you will get enough mind. If you keep enough mind, then any body job will be no problem. Also your body job, moment to moment, is the truth, and will save all people."

An eminent teacher said, "Mind is complete, then everything is complete." So if your mind is complete, then you will have no problem with any job, any action.

I think you have too much understanding. You must lose this too-much-understanding mind. Then your mind will be very simple. Then changing your job is O.K.; not changing is O.K.

Don't lose your original job. Then not only music, not only other jobs, but each step you take, each swing of your arm is already the true Dharma and saves all people.

I hope you are always keeping a mind which is clear like space, soon find your original job, get Enlightenment, and save all people from suffering.

Yours in the Dharma,
S. S.

WHAT IS YOUR JOB?

Berkeley Yong Maeng Jong Jin
September, 1977

Dear Soen Sa Nim,

The butterfly only smells the flower.
The snake hears only the heartbeat.
The golden dragon tastes only the blood.
The white swan sees the other shore.

Michael

Dear Michael,

Every animal understands its job.
Michael, what is your job?

Yours in the Dharma,
S. S.

A REPORTER'S PENPOINT

Montpelier, Vermont
February 27, 1978

Dear Soen Sa Nim,

In a house in the great city,
the master expounded the Dharma
as dogs barked and cars passed
in the night outside.

When I returned to my country home,
nothing had changed.

But the wild grasses bowed
over the chanting river.

This is the busy season of my life. I am a newspaper reporter,
covering the Vermont State Legislature. The legislature is in
session now, and my hours of work are long and irregular. As
you suggested in November, I have tried to sit every day and
have managed to do so fairly consistently. Sometimes when I
am tired, however, I sit for only a few minutes. I often wish my
life were a little less hectic, a little less constrained. I remember
very clearly my meetings with you at the Cambridge Zen
Center, and at times I wish my life were more orderly so that I
could devote more time to my family and to Zen practice.

Nonetheless, my practice continues. I believe my path is
a worthwhile one and my work is meaningful. Working with
people in a politically charged situation, dealing with important
issues, and trying to write objective, accurate news about
those issues is a good ground for practice. So I am trying.

I intend to return to the Cambridge Zen Center in the
spring for more hard training. However, I will be unable to be
with you in March as the legislature here remains in session
until early April. In the meantime, I continue sitting, working,
eating, sleeping—and not knowing. I find that your teaching
about not knowing is tremendously helpful, both in work and
in my personal life. Every now and then, that fresh breeze
blows my preconceived notions away, and I am back at the beginning, facing people, meetings, family, friends, politics,
debates, and issues anew, a HIT that comes once in a while.

At the November Yong Maeng Jong Jin, you asked me why
I was "meditating" and said I must find out why. At that time,
I said I didn't know. The reasons I continue to sit seem to
change from day to day—or perhaps minute to minute. Here
are some of those reasons:

1. I am convinced that I am literally asleep, highly unaware.
Through sitting, I have gotten some feeling about what it
would be like to be awake. I want to wake up.

2. There is a careless, forgetful, mindless side of my personality that irritates me. I want to become more mindful in my life, and I think sitting can help me to do that.

3. I want to really help people and to make the world better without finding the stain of my own personal interest on everything I do. I think practice has helped me reduce my selfishness somewhat—and can perhaps give me more accurate information about reality with which to work. So I continue to sit, meditate, practice.

And still, all of this is just thinking. Why am I sitting?

Cars go by in the street outside my office window.

It is 2:30 p.m., Monday, February 27. Time for a meeting.

Thank you for your teaching. I hope to see you in the spring.

Best wishes,
Tom

March 10, 1978

Dear Tom,

Thank you for your letter. How are you and your family?

I'm glad to hear you are sitting every day and want to practice correctly. In your letter, you said you report on the Vermont State Legislature. That is wonderful. Maybe sitting will help your reporting.

In this world there are three kinds of sharp points: the point of the pen, the tongue, and the sword. Of these three points, the sharpest is that of the pen. The written word is able to pierce where the tongue and sword cannot go. The tongue is able to pierce where a sword cannot go. The sword is the dullest of all; it is only a weapon. You are already using the point of the pen. That's wonderful! You can help many people.

But there is one point that is able to pierce where even the pen cannot go. That is the Zen point of great truth and great compassion. The other points appear and disappear; circumstances make them either necessary or useless.

Zen is before these opposites; it is the unchanging, pure and clear point. Therefore it has already pierced everything. I hope you soon get the Zen penpoint, save all beings from suffering, and get world peace.

Before, I asked you why you meditate. You gave me three reasons—not good, not bad. I think many words are not necessary. Zen is turning a complicated mind into a simple mind. If you have a simple mind, you can do everything, and you have no hindrance anywhere. So, your sitting means understanding yourself, which means getting Enlightenment and saving all beings. But your answer says, "I am here; something is there." If you keep this mind, you cannot attain the truth.

If you want to attain the truth, you must have a revolution in your mind. Communism is only an outside revolution. Zen is an inside and outside revolution. If you have an inside and outside revolution, then there is no subject, no object. Inside and outside become one. When you see the sky, only blue. When you see the trees, only green. When you are doing something, you must *do* it. Don't make two; don't make one. Then you already have world peace and complete freedom. That is keeping your correct situation moment to moment.

If the world's politicians kept this mind, then there would be no fighting, no suffering, and they would help each other on the Bodhisattva path. This is possible. But they usually only keep I-my-me, so the world has many problems. You must teach them. Use your Zen penpoint.

You already said why you are sitting: "Cars go by in the street outside my office window. It is 2:30 p.m., Monday, February 27. Time for a meeting." That is wonderful. But your answer is very late. So I say to you, the arrow has already passed downtown. Again, I ask you: Why do you sit? Tell me! Tell me! Many words are not necessary. Only one point is very important.

Your poem is very wonderful. Here is a poem for you:

Dogs barked and cars passed
In the night outside.
Spoken Dharma is already a mistake— 10,000 miles
   away—
In a temple in the great city.

Wild grasses bowed
Over the chanting river.
Changing, changing, just like this
When I returned to my original home.

Yours in the Dharma,
S. S.

III. ON RELATIONSHIPS

FOUR KINDS OF ANGER

Berkeley, California
November 4, 1976

Dear Soen Sa Nim,

How are you, and how is it to be back East again? We miss you here! I hope the seven-day Yong Maeng Jong Jin is going well.

It is strange how things happen, sometimes backwards. I felt very clear after the Yong Maeng Jong Jin you conducted (even though *during* the weekend I thought all the dry-cleaning in the world would not get my mind clear!). But two days ago I suddenly found myself *screaming* mad at my son to the point that I even tried to slap him. I felt just terrible that, after going to three Yong Maeng Jong Jins in five weeks' time, sitting every day, etc., I could revert to such a totally angry mind. And over such a small thing! I went to my room and lay on my bed and started to cry in despair at myself—and then an odd thing happened. I realized that something very important had just happened and crying was not the answer.

I realized that it was time to stop worrying and feeling guilty about him and DO something to change his environment and therefore his karma. Right now he is in a very poor environment; school is not challenging, this home is not making him grow, his friends are getting into trouble and not interested in much except excitement. He has always resisted every effort to change school or to move or whatever—and I always have given in, perhaps feeling I didn't really know the "right" answer anyway or perhaps afraid he would reject me.

This time I saw what had to be done, clear as clear: he needs to go to a good school for at least a while, whether he likes it or not, whether he hates me for it or not. I saw that I was willing to be "100%," finally—even if I turned out to be "wrong." I think I really surprised him—because I got up off my bed and walked into the kitchen where he was and *told* him all that—and also that I was no longer willing to let him push my anger button like that.

At first he just said "no" loud and clear. But for once I did not waver but told him that I felt very strongly he should give it a try—what did he have to lose? And I told him that unless he could begin to challenge himself to try something new, he would never experience much in his life.

Just before we sat Zen last night, he came in and told me he had changed his mind and would go to the school for a day and see what he thought.

I feel *so good*, Soen Sa Nim. I just wanted to share this with you very much. It has so much to do with the "dropping ashes on the Buddha" kong-an ("Mind Meal," Sixth Gate): Somebody comes to the Zen Center, smoking a cigarette. He blows smoke and drops ashes on the Buddha. If you are standing there at that time, what can you do? I feel as if I am making some progress toward attaining an "answer" to it . . . which seems (for me anyway) to have to do with that thing you keep telling us, that "Zen is believing 100% in yourself," something I have just *never* been able to do. I've discovered that I believe 100% in my love for my son, to the point that I am willing for him to reject me or even for my idea to fail. He's just not old enough to make total decisions for his life in every way. This is one I have to make *for* him. And evidently he went inside himself, knew I was right in his heart, and decided to go along with it.

Anyway—he is a different kid today, and whatever happens, yesterday was perhaps a turning point for us both.

Your teaching is beginning to get through to me, Soen Sa Nim—thank you very much.

Love,
Diana

Dear Diana,

Thank you for your letter. How are you and Ezra and all your family? We have just finished the seven-day Yong Maeng Jong Jin here at the Providence Zen Center.

After sitting Yong Maeng Jong Jin, your mind was clear. A clear mind is like a clear mirror, so when anger appeared, you reflected with angry action. You love your son, so you were angry. Is this correct? Don't check your mind—when you are angry, be angry. Afterwards, checking is no good.

Your previous anger and the anger you talked about in your letter are different. Before Yong Maeng Jong Jin, it was attached anger; after Yong Maeng Jong Jin, your anger was only reflected anger. If you do more hard training, the reflected anger will change to perceived anger. After more practicing, perceived anger will disappear. Then you will have only loving anger—inside you will not be angry, only angry on the outside. So attached anger, reflected anger, perceived anger, loving anger—all are changing, changing, changing. Anger is anger; anger is the truth. Don't worry, don't check yourself—it has already passed. How you keep just-now mind is very important.

Attached anger sometimes lasts for three hours, sometimes three days, and does not quickly return to love-mind. When you were crying, you had reflected anger; it did not last long. Soon you returned to your mind that loves your son, and you knew what to do to help him. You believed in yourself 100%. After more hard training, your reflected anger will change to perceived anger. You will feel anger but not show it; you will be able to control your mind. Finally, you will have only loving anger, anger only on the outside to help other people—"You must do this!"—but no anger on the inside. This is true love-mind.

You had already done three days of hard training during Yong Maeng Jong Jin, so your mind light was shining to your son's mind. Everything is from a primary cause; primary cause means karma. If your karma disappears, then the primary cause disappears. If the primary cause disappears, then the result will disappear. Your son's bad karma and your karma are closely connected, so if your karma disappears, then your son's karma will also disappear. This is your mind's light shining to your son's mind.

It is like sharing the same T.V. station and the same channel. If the original station changes the picture, all the pictures on the same channel will also change. Buddha said, "If one mind is pure, then the universe becomes pure." So if your mind is pure, your world will be pure. Your world means your family, your friends, your country—all of them. So changing your son's school is a very good idea. Sometimes, when the situation is bad, everything is bad; when the situation changes, then it is possible to change everything.

So, your mind light is already shining to your son's mind in great love. Great love means believing in yourself 100%. Then everything is no problem. I read your letter, and I also felt very good. All this is from your strong practicing.

You must finish your homework. Somebody comes to the Zen Center, smokes a cigarette, blows smoke and drops ashes on the Buddha. How do you fix the cigarette-man's mind? How do you correct him? Quickly, quickly, answer me!

I hope you only go straight—don't know, keep a mind which is clear like space, finish your homework, attain Enlightenment and great love mind, and save all beings from suffering.

Yours in the Dharma,
S. S.

THE GREAT WORK OF LIFE AND DEATH

Boulder, Colorado
August 12, 1977

Dear Soen Sa Nim,

Your letter, newsletter, and picture made me cry—and I am so grateful. I understand: straightforward mind, straightforward heart, straightforward speech, straightforward body.

My father died yesterday. I built a small altar in my room and sat, and I told him to recognize that all things are in his own mind—his original brightness. Too late, I was finally able to say, "I love you." I am thankful to have your picture on the altar.

Thank you for your great kindness.

Yours,
Sheldon

August 18, 1977

Dear Sheldon,

Thank you for your letter. How are you?

In your letter, you told me that your father died. I grieve for you.

Long ago in China when the great Zen Master Nam Cheon died, his students and all those who knew him were very sad. The custom at that time was to go to the dead person's house and cry, "*Aigo! Aigo! Aigo!*" But when the Zen Master's best student, a layman named Bu Dae Sa, heard of his teacher's death, he went to Nam Cheon's temple, opened the door, stood in front of the coffin, and laughed, "HA HA HA HA!!"— great laughter.

The many people who were assembled to mourn Nam Cheon's death were surprised at this laughter. The temple Housemaster said, "You were our teacher's best student. Our teacher has died, and everyone is sad. Why are you laughing?"

Bu Dae Sa said, "You say our master has died. Where did he go?" The Housemaster was silent. He could not answer.

Then Bu Dae Sa said, "You don't understand where our teacher went, so I am very sad. *Aigo! Aigo! Aigo!*"

You must understand this. What does this mean? If you have no answer, I grieve for you.

Zen is the great work of life and death. What is life? What is death? When you attain this, then everything is clear, everything is complete, and everything is freedom.

Let's say we have a glass of water. Now its temperature is about 60°. If you reduce the temperature to 20°, it becomes ice. If you raise the temperature above 212°, it will become steam. As the temperature changes, H_2O in the form of water appears and disappears, but H_2O does not appear and does not disappear. Ice, water, and steam are only its form. Name and form change, but H_2O does not change. If you understand the temperature, then you understand the form. Your true self is like this.

But what is your true self? Your body has life and death. But your true self has no life, no death. You think, "My body is me." This is not correct. This is crazy. You must wake up!

Steam, ice, and water are all H_2O; but if you are attached to water, and the water becomes ice, then you say the water disappeared. So it is dead! Raise the temperature; the water is born again! Raise the temperature again; the water disappears and becomes steam, and the water is again dead!

On the Zen Circle [Appendix V] this is the area from 0° to 90°. If you are attached to something and it disappears, you suffer. If you are attached to only doing what you like, you suffer. Don't be attached to water, O.K.? Being attached to water is being attached to form. Form and name are always changing, changing, changing, nonstop. So form and name are emptiness. Another way to say this is that form is emptiness, emptiness is form. This understanding is 90° on the Zen Circle.

But name and form are made by thinking. Water does not say, "I am water." Steam does not say, "I am steam." If you cut off all thinking, are you and the water the same or different? "Same" and "different" are made by your thinking. How can you answer? There is no form, no emptiness—no words. This is 180° on the Zen Circle. If you open your mouth, you have already made a mistake.

If you cut off all thinking, you will see everything just as it is. Without thinking, water is water; ice is ice; steam is steam. No ideas hinder you. Then your correct relationship to H_2O in any form appears by itself. We call this "just-like-this." This is 360° on the Zen Circle. Just-like-this mind is clear mind. Clear mind has no I-my-me. Without I-my-me you can perceive your correct relationship to H_2O and use it without desire for yourself. You will not suffer when water disappears and becomes ice or steam.

Your father's original face has no death and no life. His body appears and disappears but his Dharma body does not appear and does not disappear. You must recognize that all things are in your own mind. Just this is finding your true self. Great love, great compassion, and the great Bodhisattva way come from this attainment. You must find this.

I hope you only go straight—don't know, soon find your father's original face, get Enlightenment, and save all beings from suffering.

Yours in the Dharma,
S. S.

TEACHING A DAUGHTER

Providence, Rhode Island
September 20, 1977

Dear Soen Sa Nim, Teacher,

I have been struggling with a conflict. I wanted very much to write and talk with you, but I wanted to be able to say something crystalline.

Still, I knew if I waited that long, I might be a grandmother. So I swallow my Zen-ego in a gulp and write you my words after thoughts.

For my homework, you gave me Hyang Eom's "Up a Tree" ("Mind Meal," Fifth Gate). Answer: If someone asked me such a dumb question while I was hanging by my teeth, I would have to kick him and make him stop plaguing me with questions.

My practice is going fine, which means I am struggling like hell. Sometimes I am in such a turmoil that I find myself in the Zen Center in the middle of the day, sitting. One day Bobby and I had a good talk about bringing my thirteen-year-old daughter to sit at the Center. This is very difficult, because she is much like an eighteen-year-old in her set of mind and her emotional development. I don't want to turn her off from Zen for good, but I feel strongly that she should begin. I have never introduced her to any religion, simply saying that when she was old enough, she could choose her own. But now, will I be going back on my word if I want her to start sitting?

All my love to you,
Leslie

Dear Leslie,

How are you and your family? Thank you for your letter.

About your homework ("Mind Meal," Fifth Gate). You are hanging from a branch by your teeth. Your kong-an answer is only your idea. Your feet are tied—how can you kick? In this kong-an only a one-pointed action is necessary. This action is already beyond life and death. If you're attached to staying alive, then you have a problem.

You talked about your daughter and about saying to your daughter, "You must decide." This is very difficult. Often a hundred-year-old man cannot choose what is correct, so how can a thirteen-year-old choose the correct way? If you want to talk to your daughter about Zen, you might say, "I like Zen. I like other religions too, but for me Zen makes sense, so I practice Zen. Come to meditation practice one time at the Zen Center. Try it; if you don't like it, that's O.K."

With children from twelve to seventeen years old, anything can come into their consciousness. They want very much to understand, and they have strong emotions and strong intellect, but not such a strong will. So they cannot decide. So, you must speak correctly to your daughter. Tell her why Zen is important to you. Also, talk to her about what it is to be human, what the world is, what karma is, what good and bad are. You must explain these things to her; this age is a very important age because she is open to learn. If you teach her the correct direction at this time, it will help her choose a path that is not only I-my-me. You must use your close karma with your daughter and teach her. That is a mother's job. Only "you decide" is not enough.

If you keep a thinking mind, then your everyday life will be a dream and you won't be able to teach your daughter correct moment-to-moment action. If you wake up then you can use your strong karma together to teach your daughter the true way. Here is a wake-up story about a teacher and a student who had very close karma.

Five hundred years ago in Korea there was a very rich and famous sutra master. At that time, monks from wealthy families inherited money, and they paid for their students to go to sutra school. Rich monks had many students and poor monks had very few. The sutra master in this story had 100 students. The one-hundredth was a young monk named Dol Um. Dol Um was given money to learn the sutras, and he studied hard for three years. Then he thought, "These sutras are not necessary. All sutras only save your mind. If your mind is empty, of what use are the sutras?" He understood that he had to practice at a Zen temple. So the young monk spoke to his teacher. "Master, only reading sutras is no good. We must go to a Zen temple. You are old and will soon die. Where will you go?"

"I don't know," answered the sutra master. "You are right. We will go. But who will take care of my land, my barns, my possessions?"

"You have many capable students. Leave everything with them."

"O.K., then. It is decided. We will leave tomorrow."

None of the other monks was like this one. They only thought, "I want to be rich; I want to be a famous sutra master." But the one-hundredth monk was very clever. His teacher thought, "Ah, I decided to stop at one hundred students, and Buddha has helped me by sending this especially clever boy. It is good to follow his direction."

There was a meeting of the whole monastery at which the teacher announced that he would be going to the Zen temple with his young student. Then he told everyone to take care of his rice fields and large barns, assigning each monk some responsibility. Early the next day, they packed provisions, said goodbye, and left for the Zen temple. After walking about three miles up the mountainside, they stopped to rest and drink some tea. Looking down at the monastery in a valley, the student noticed a fire. "Master, look, a fire. What is burning?"

"Oh no! It is my barn! You go on alone. I must return to the temple!"

"But Master, soon you will die. Where are you going?"

"I must go back!"

So the sutra master returned to his monastery. Dol Um realized that his teacher had many attachments and that he could not change his mind. He went straight on to the Zen temple.

Three years passed. The famous sutra master died, and the news of his death spread. The traditional ceremony forty-nine days after his death was planned, with a thousand guests expected. Many monks came to share the food, the drink and the master's money. Dol Um too came to the funeral ceremony. He was met by a Dharma brother, the head monk, who said, "You're no good. When the master was dying, you did not visit him. You're coming now just to get a share of the property."

Dol Um said, "No, I don't want any land or money. I would like two pots of rice soup, please, if this is possible."

"Only this?"

"Yes."

"O.K."

It was the custom to make an offering of food to the local demons so that they would be afraid to trespass on the ceremonial grounds. So Dol Um took the soup to a large field outside the funeral area in which there were large rocks for milling rice. Then he entered the innermost Dharma room of the temple and hit a column three times. Immediately a large snake appeared, went outside to the rocks, and drank all the rice soup.

"Teacher," said Dol Um, "why did you get this body?"

The snake said, "I am sorry. I should have listened to you. Now I have a snake's body."

Why a snake? He had had a great forty-ninth-day funeral ceremony and had only received a snake's body! His consciousness was like that of a snake, so he received a snake's body. Then the snake began to cry.

Dol Um said, "Teacher, you have many desires. You have eaten all this soup, yet it was not enough. This snake's body is not good for you. It is only a desire body. You must hit your head against the rocks and get rid of this body!"

The snake replied, "Oh, this body is not so bad; I cannot!"

"You must try!" Only silence. "You must try!" Then Dol Um hit the snake three times and killed it.

A cloud of blue smoke rose from the snake carcass and floated away. Dol Um followed it. A bird flew nearby, and the cloud began to assume its form. "No good!" shouted Dol Um. Again it floated on and began to enter the form of a cow. "No good!" he shouted again. Then the cloud floated farther and father into the mountains, deep into the mountains to a little house where a middle-aged couple lived. The cloud entered the house.

Four years later, Dol Um went back to the house in the woods. He asked the couple about the health of their three-year-old son. The couple was shocked. They had never seen this monk before. How did he know they had a young son? And as it turned out, their son was deathly ill. Dol Um asked to see the young boy. As soon as Dol Um picked up the boy he became healthy and very happy.

Dol Um said, "Please give me your son. If you do not, he will again become very ill and he will die." The couple hesitated, but then they agreed. They could see the monk and their son had very close karma together.

One day when the boy was five years old, Dol Um said, "Now it is time for you to understand yourself."

"Yes, sir. How?"

Dol Um led him to a rice-paper window in which there was a tiny hole. "You must sit here and look at this hole until a big cow comes through it. Only this. Don't think about anything. Only watch for a big cow. When it comes, you will understand your true self."

So, at the small temple in the mountains, the child only ate, slept, and looked through the hole in the rice paper. "When will the cow come?" His very clear child's mind held only this question. One day passed, two days, almost one hundred days, then the hole grew bigger and bigger, and a huge cow appeared—"Mooooo!"

The boy cried out, "Master! Master! The cow! The cow has come!"

Dol Um rushed over and slapped his face. "Where is the cow?"

"Oh!" The child understood himself completely, and attained Enlightenment. Then he looked at his teacher and said, "You were my student before!"

"Yes, sir," said Dol Um, bowing.

So wake up! This child woke up early. In his previous life he had many desires, so he could not wake up. Dol Um liked him and cared for him; he understood his teacher's mind. Dol Um helped his teacher and chose a good rebirth; he had patience and understood how to help the young boy open his mind.

The hundredth student and his teacher had very good karma, so in the next life they were again teacher and student. Mothers and daughters have strong karma together too—lifetime after lifetime. This is interesting. Having the same karma is very important. But having a strong direction is most important. Before Dol Um studied at the Zen temple he could not use his karma with his teacher; after he understood himself, he understood his teacher's mind as well. So first you must find your true way, understand your karma, then use the strong karma you have with your daughter, your family and friends, and with other people to help them. Then you will be able to save all beings.

I hope you only go straight—don't know, wake up, give your daughter correct teaching, and save all beings from suffering.

Yours in the Dharma,
S. S.

I CAN NO LONGER FOLLOW MY HUSBAND

Los Angeles, California
July 7, 1978

Dear Soen Sa Nim,

Last night my husband came to see me and we had a long talk. At first I was very sad and felt terrible because he asked me to make a choice: if I love him then I must give up Buddhist meditation except for once a week, follow him and be a "normal" wife. Yes, I love him—he has great goodness and a loving heart. I will always adore him and help him any way I can if he needs me. So what to do? What to do?

I made a decision some time back that I must cultivate the Buddha Dharma 100% now, and no matter what, I cannot turn back.

I understand my husband's needs and his desire for a companion, but I can no longer follow his way, spending every weekend at the seashore while he is fishing. By chance I opened *Dropping Ashes on the Buddha* to page 17. There were your words saying—have great faith, great courage, and a great question. So, I said to myself this morning, put it all down—my husband, my desire, my attachment, is this correct or not correct? and so on—let it go! Just "only go straight." Now, I really don't understand anything at all, I must admit, and sometimes I hear myself say, "What is this all about?" I sure don't know—

All I can do is only keep "Kwan Seum Bosal, Kwan Seum Bosal, Kwan Seum Bosal," from moment to moment.

I'll move into the Zen Center full-time by September. We all think of you and miss you.

Yours in the Dharma,
Sumana

Dear Sumana,

Thank you for your letter. How are you?

I read your letter. Your decision is very clear and strong. So I say to you, "Wonderful, wonderful!" But being a Bodhisattva means when people come, don't cut them off; when people go, don't cut them off. This is living with no hindrance, which is already saving all people.

There are four kinds of Bodhisattva action. The first is generosity—just giving people what they need or want. The next is good speech—giving encouragement, confidence, and a persevering mind. Next is telling them about the Dharma and the way out of suffering. Finally, if they don't listen, you must act together with them—together action. Whether it is bad or good action doesn't matter; your not-moving center shines to their minds. Then someday they will ask for help and listen.

If you have strong Dharma energy, then these four kinds of action are possible. But if your Dharma energy is not strong, together action is not possible. So, if it is not possible, then first it is most important to make your center strong, get Enlightenment, and get strong Dharma energy. Then you can try these four kinds of Bodhisattva action, and then you can save your husband and all beings.

You said you will be living at the Zen Center full-time in September. That means you understand that your energy is not strong enough to save your husband; you see that your correct way is to become strong yourself. That is wonderful! Someday your energy will become strong, and you can save your husband.

Two days ago, I played with some magnets in our library at lunch time. Plus and plus cannot come together. Minus and plus come together very strongly. All things in the universe are like that. You and your husband like some things about each other and don't like some things about each other. You want the True Way, but your husband wants to go fishing: you are like magnets. But if your husband truly loves you 100%, he will perceive why you want to practice Zen and why killing is no good. Then he will stop going fishing and will follow you.

You understand all of this, so you have decided to live full-time at the Zen Center. That is called the way of Kwan Seum Bosal. Already, you are trying Kwan Seum Bosal. That is the Great Bodhisattva Way; you already have saved your husband. This medicine has already gone into him. You don't know yet if it's working or not, but someday, it will work. So I hope you only go straight—Kwan Seum Bosal, don't check your mind or feelings, get Enlightenment, and save all beings from suffering.

Yours in the Dharma,
S. S.

THROW AWAY YOUR ZEN MIND

Philadelphia, Pennsylvania
July 28, 1978

Dear Soen Sa Nim,

Hello. How are you? Thank you for your marvelous letter. Right now Stan is in France. I miss him a lot, but he will be back soon.

This letter expresses my concern for my parents so it is hard to write. There is a lot of bad karma between me and my mother, and I find it hard to see clearly what is going on.

As you know, my family is Jewish. When I was a child this didn't seem very important. Nearly everyone I knew was Jewish, so being Jewish wasn't special. My mother only went to temple when she had to, and while my father was a cantor in a temple, he also had his own private religion in his head. So when I grew up and moved away, I didn't practice Judaism, and I certainly didn't believe in the doctrines. It was just there in my background, like having brown hair.

Both my brother and I have chosen non-Jewish spouses. This is very hard for my parents and for my mother's family to accept. Luckily, they like Stan a lot so, while they will not mention our marriage to their friends, they are happy to visit with us—although no visit with them can really be called happy. The whole situation is very confused by the bad karma between my mother and me and between my mother and father.

My Zen practice is very painful to them. I can never tell them about taking the Precepts. They see my involvement with Zen as turning my back on my people. Jews have been persecuted for thousands of years, and when a Jew adopts another religion, it is considered the act of a traitor. I have told them that I have not taken on another God opposed to their God, but they don't really believe this. So they feel pain and shame. They feel they have not done their job right. They believe that if they had done their job right, then I would be a good Jewish woman married to a good Jewish man, raising lots of good Jewish kids. So, instead of taking pleasure in Stan being such a wonderful man, or in my having such a good job, or simply in the fact that I am far nicer and happier than I used to be, they ask themselves what they have done wrong to have a daughter who studies Zen.

The symbol for all these feelings, of course, is the wedding. They are very upset about a Buddhist ceremony. They will not come, and I think it is right that they should not come since they are so upset. But also, they want another ceremony, and they insist that this ceremony come before the Buddhist ceremony. This is very important to them. I have trouble understanding this until I think of how important it is to me that the Buddhist ceremony be the first one. So Stan and I have agreed to a ceremony by a justice of the peace, with only my parents present, in late March. Then my mother will be able to say she was present at her daughter's wedding. She sees this as part of my duty to her.

I have tried to explain my beliefs to my family and to my relatives. My father understood, but none of the others could even hear my words. They were too frightened by something that is outside their tradition. Anything outside their tradition carries the seeds of apostasy, and listening to it is dangerous.

Nevertheless, Stan and I are very honored to have you come here and give a Dharma talk and perform our true Buddhist marriage ceremony. Other people in the sangha here are also very honored that you will visit. I am sorry that my own mind has been so muddied by my family situation. I hope it becomes clear.

Tonight when sitting I saw myself walking towards a doorway, only I was standing in the way.

Much love,
Judy

August 6, 1978

Dear Judy,

Thank you for your letter. How are you and Stan?

I read your letter. I understand your mind. I also understand your parents' mind. Both are correct. You have your opinion. Your parents have their opinion. Your opinion and your parents' opinion are in conflict, so you have a problem. If you make your opinion disappear, then there will be no problem. That is Zen. Then your mind will be very wide and can take care of your parents' opinion. But if you keep your opinion, you cannot take care of your parents' ideas. When your opinion disappears, your mind will be clear like space, and you can digest any idea, any opinion.

You talk about your family and your wedding.

You and Stan are already strong Zen students. But, Zen mind is not Zen mind. That is, if you are attached to Zen mind, then you have a problem, and your way is very narrow. Throwing away Zen mind is correct Zen mind. Only keep the question, "What is the best way of helping other people?" If your wedding is only for you, then you are holding onto your idea, in the same way that your mother holds her idea. But if you keep the mind, "My wedding is only for all people," then this mind is already beyond time and space, life and death, good and bad, likes and dislikes.

Your parents want a justice of the peace ceremony in late March. It doesn't matter whether this occurs before or after the Buddhist ceremony. What is most important? Moment to moment, how do you keep just-now mind? That is most important. If you keep just-now mind, then you can keep your correct situation and help other people moment to moment. This is called great love, great compassion, and the great Bodhisattva way.

You and Stan both have advanced educations and respectable jobs. You are also high-class Zen students. So your ideas, your jobs, and your practice are already helping other people. But you are attached to Zen, so you have the same kind of narrow opinion that your mother has. Put down that mind. If you help other people, then two ceremonies, three ceremonies, a hundred ceremonies, a thousand ceremonies are possible. Why not? First, follow your parents' idea. But don't lose your correct direction. Then following their idea is the truth. The great way has no gate. The tongue has no bone. I have already told you this.

All of this is not an accident, not a coincidence; it is happening by natural process. So don't worry about anything! Only help your parents. If you have a child who cries a lot and behaves badly, give it candy. Then the child will stop crying and will be very happy. You must give your parents Dharma-candy. Then they will not cry. And slowly, slowly, teach your parents. Don't use words; only use your actions. If you lose your mouth, you will lose your way. Be very careful.

So what is a daughter's responsibility? When you are with your parents, keep 100%-helping-your-parents mind. Helping your parents is very necessary. When you are with Stan, keep a wife's mind 100%. Moment to moment, keep your correct situation. Any outside action is no problem—why do you do that action? If "why" is clear, then any action is already great Bodhisattva action. So don't make Zen a narrow way. There is no gate, no path, so any way and Zen's way become one.

If you correctly understand Zen, you understand your true self. If you understand your true self, and if you are Christian, then correct Christianity is possible; if you are Jewish, correct Judaism is possible. If Communists sit Zen, correct Communism is possible. If people are attached to their opinions, they cannot find correct Christianity, Judaism, or Communism.

Your mother makes Judaism narrow. But God made everything. Any way is God's way; everything has God-nature. Then God's way is very wide and has no hindrance. So if you correctly teach everyday mind, then maybe your mother will open her mind and understand your actions and your mind. Then for you and your mother, for you and your whole family, there will be no problem.

I hope you only go straight—don't know, throw away your Zen mind, get Enlightenment, and save all beings from suffering.

Yours in the Dharma,
S. S.

IV. QUESTIONS ABOUT SUFFERING

THE HUMAN ROUTE

New York, New York
May 15, 1978

Dear Seung Sahn Soen Sa,

I don't think you will know me, because I have seen you only a few times. I attended a Kido with you last summer. However, I hope you will be able to give me some advice.

Last month my younger sister Pam died in a very strange and lonely way. The karma of my family is difficult and full of confusion and pain. Pam was paralyzed from the waist down for a year and a half. She tried to kill herself jumping from a balcony and broke her spine in three places. I cry as I write this. Though I was close to her before, I became much closer after that, going to Texas to visit her, talking with her, writing many letters. I loved her very much. She had a very beautiful heart, very loving and seeking. Then last month she suddenly ran away in her car (she had a special car that she could drive). She drove up to northern Texas, called my mother twice, and then we didn't hear from her for many days. She was finally found in the woods by the police. She had tried to get out of her car into her wheelchair, fell to the ground, dragged herself into the woods, built a fire and died there—probably from exposure and starvation.

For myself, these last years have also been a struggle; I was in a mental hospital twice and the past three years have been a journey back to a normal mind. It is so terribly sad to me because, just when I was begining to be really strong for her, to be able to truly help her, she is gone—and I think she had much pain and anger in her heart when she died.

I have her ashes now on my altar, and I feel strong energy from them. I guess I wish to ask you two things. First, what can I do for her now? I try to find her when I sit Zen. I think of her always—it sometimes seems as if I feel her suffering—and every night I chant, but this doesn't seem enough. I want so badly to see her, though I know I can't, to help her wherever she is, to reach her somehow and make sure she is not suffering.

Secondly, please tell me how to purify myself and my family when there are so many difficult things. I myself am such a beginner on the spiritual path—part of the reason I went crazy was because I thought I was such a bad person. I know somewhat differently now, but could you explain a little to me about karma with much suffering and unhappiness?

I will be deeply, deeply grateful to you for any words that you can send me. As I write this letter, the tears come from inside with my sorrow and my desire to bring love where there is so much pain.

Yours in Kanzeon,
Sheila

May 27, 1978

Dear Sheila,

Thank you for your letter. How are you? I read your letter and I am also very sad. I understand your mind; I understand your thoughts about your sister. I understand your love for your sister. You and your sister have very strong karma, same karma. So when your sister dies, your mind also dies.

But that is all feeling. If you are holding your feelings, you cannot help your sister. Also, you cannot help yourself or your family. Let your feelings be! You must find your correct way; then your mind can shine to your sister and to your family. Then in the next life this sadness will not appear. But if you are only holding these sad feelings, in your next life this same sadness will appear.

Everything is from a primary cause and leads to a result. An action in your past life gives you a result in this life. If in this life you do not make this feeling disappear, then it will become a primary cause and in the next life there will again be the same result. The name for this is samsara. Many people do not understand this, so they are attached to a result. Because of this, when they are very sad and crying, they suffer.

If you understand karma, you will not hold onto the result, so your mind will not be tight and suffering. Crying time, only cry. When that is finished, it is finished. You must keep a clear mind. Then you will make clear, correct karma.

So don't hold onto your feelings, don't make anything, don't be attached to anything. Put it all down! Then your mind will become clear and your mind light will shine everywhere. That is called Dharma energy. Then your mind will shine to your sister and the rest of your family. Then the primary cause will disappear and this suffering and sadness will not appear again.

The Human Route

Coming empty-handed, going empty-handed—
    that is human.
When you are born, where do you come from?
When you die, where do you go?
Life is like a floating cloud which appears.
Death is like a floating cloud which disappears.
The floating cloud itself originally does not exist.
Life and death, coming and going, are also like this.
But there is one thing which always remains clear.
It is pure and clear, not depending on life and death.
Then what is the one pure and clear thing?

You must attain this true self which is not dependent on life or death, which always remains clear and pure. Then you will see your sister's original face and you will save yourself, your sister, and your family.

If you don't understand the one pure and clear thing, then only go straight—don't know. Let everything be! Only try, try, try for 10,000 years nonstop. This is very important.

You said that you were in a mental hospital. That is very difficult. Controlling your mind when you are alone and practicing alone may also be very difficult. The best thing is for you to go to a Zen Center; practicing together with others is very important. When you are bowing together, sitting together, eating together, chanting together, and working together with other people, everybody helps you control your bad karma. Then it is easy to completely put down your opinion, your condition, and your situation.

Good and bad are your true teachers. But living by yourself, you don't understand good and bad. You cannot see your bad karma. So your bad karma always controls you, and your problem is nonstop. If you want your bad karma to disappear, please come to a Zen Center.

You want to know how to help your sister. I already told you, but if you want to do something special, Buddhism has a mantra for dead people: Ji Jang Bosal. Try Ji Jang Bosal 3,000 times a day for forty-nine days. Then your sister will be born again in a good body.

I hope you only go straight—don't know: don't check your feelings, your mind, or your understanding, find the true way and save your sister, your family, and all beings from suffering.

Yours in the Dharma,
S. S.

IN THIS WORLD EVERYBODY IS CRAZY

Berkeley, California
January 25, 1978

Dear Soen Sa Nim,

I have a question for you. I work every day with crazy kids who scream and yell obscenities and are very self-destructive. One girl even bites her own arm and makes it sore. One theory about this illness is that these people are possessed by the spirit of a dead person.

Is this correct? How can I help them?

I love you,
Marge

January 25, 1978

Dear Marge,

Hello. How are you?

You spoke in your letter about crazy children and one crazy girl you work with. This girl is like a moth that flies into a flame, burns its body, and dies. In this world everyone is a little like this, so everyone is crazy.

One of my students works in a Jewish nursing home. A few days ago, a man set a fire there. When the police came, they asked the man why he set the fire. He said, "I don't like this place." The police checked their records and found that the man had set several fires, all at Jewish-owned stores. When they asked him why, he said, "I don't know why I don't like Jewish people. I just set fires." This is crazy.

Both the children you work with and this man are like moths—they are strongly attached to something, so they do the same action over and over without knowing why. A mind that goes narrowly on one track like this is crazy. If a person's mind is a little wider, it is not so crazy. Wider still, it is only a little crazy sometimes. If your mind is clear like space, then you are completely sane.

When people hold on to their thinking and follow their thinking, they are controlled by their habits so they do the same action over and over and they create their own suffering. If you hang on to your opinions, your condition, and your situation, you too are like a moth. If you cut through your opinions, your condition and your situation, then there is no life and no death.

How do you keep your correct situation moment to moment? In other words, how do you help other people? If somebody is hungry, what do you do? If somebody hurts himself, what can you do? You already understand. Don't check your feelings; don't check your mind; don't check anything—only help people. If you cut off all thinking and keep this mind, "How can I help?" the correct action will appear. That is great love, great compassion, and the great Bodhisattva way. This is our original job. If you hold onto your opinion, your condition, and your situation, you create opposites—"I" and "they"—and then you cannot help other people.

If you don't make anything and don't hold onto anything, your mind is already absolute. There is no subject and no object. Inside and outside become one. Everything is true as it is. Then your everyday life is the truth, your moment to moment situation is correct, and already you have saved all beings from suffering. If you keep this mind, you will know how to help the crazy girl and the other crazy children you work with.

So I hope you only go straight—don't know and keep a great Bodhisattva vow, get Enlightenment, and save all beings from suffering.

Yours in the Dharma,
S. S.

A THREE-YEAR RETREAT

New Haven, Connecticut
September 20, 1977

Dear Soen Sa Nim,

I am still in bed, and although I don't have pain any more, I still have a problem with my leg. It's numb from the knee down, so I think that I'll have to do something besides only rest to fix my back problem. Do you know why someone would have an extra vertebra or different bone structure in each hip?

This time in bed has been like a retreat in many ways. For the first time in my life, I understand that I have no choices to make. People bring me food—I can't choose. I can't do what I feel like doing. Every day just comes and goes. People come and go. Sometimes it's warm, sometimes it's cold. I just have to stay here and let everything occur just the way it does, and I must keep my mind clear. There is no choice; I cannot act out my karma. So this sickness is very strong teaching. I understand something I never did before: if you are dependent on anything, you make suffering. It's funny, because I am dependent on everyone, but at the same time my mind is not dependent.

I hope you are well. Much love to you.

Yours in the Dharma,
Andrea

October 5, 1977

Dear Andrea,

Hello. Thank you for your letter.

In your letter, you said that you have no choice about any food or any action, and that you are dependent on everyone, but that your mind is not dependent on anything. That is wonderful. This is correct Zen sickness: sick time, only sick. No choice, no checking, not dependent, only sick. Then sick is not sick. This is high-class practice and a high-class education.

Do you know this story about Bu Sol Go Sa? He was a monk who wanted to do a three-year retreat with two monk friends. On the way to the mountains, he got married. A girl came running up to the three monks and cried, "If I don't marry, I will kill myself." So Bu Sol Go Sa did Bodhisattva action and married her. His two friends said, "You are only filled with desire. This is not the action of a Bodhisattva but of a selfish man." After many more accusing and angry words, the two monks went on their way.

Just after his marriage, Bu Sol Go Sa became very sick. Just like you, he could not move. His wife was very kind to him. She did everything for him—washed his body, brought him food. Every day for three years he could only lie in bed and look at the ceiling.

The two monks finished their three-year retreat and were returning home. They thought about their Dharma friend. They decided to visit him, and when they reached his house, they found his wife sweeping the front yard. The two monks said, "Hello. How are you? Where is your husband?"

"My husband has been sick for three years. He is so sick that he cannot do anything."

One monk whispered to the other, "This is his bad karma—he broke the Precepts and got married, so he got sick for three years." But they wanted to see their Dharma friend, so they asked if they could visit him for a while. Although the wife was a little angry inside, she acted kindly and showed the monks into her husband's room. They went in and started laughing. "So, you have been sick for three years. Not bad!"

When Bu Sol Go Sa saw them, he got up. "Oh, how are you? Thank you very much for visiting me."

They were startled. "We heard that you have been sick for three years. How can you get up?"

He said, "Maybe I can get up because you did strong practicing for three years."

Then they said, "Maybe. We worried about you every day."

"I had so much bad karma that for three years I was sick. But you did hard training all the time. What was your practice? Please teach me. What did you get?"

The two monks said, "Oh, we read many sutras and the speech of many eminent teachers, so we understand all Buddha's teachings." For the next few hours, they told him what they had learned.

Finally, Bu Sol Go Sa said, "Yes, you understand Buddha's speech very well. What is Buddha's mind?"

"Buddha's mind?"

"Yes, what is Buddha's mind?"

"Do you know Buddha's mind?"

"Well, I think if you have Buddha's mind, anything is possible. So, we'll try something." Then he called his wife and asked her to help him.

She brought three long thin-necked bottles with wide bottoms, filled with water. Then Bu Sol Go Sa took three pieces of rope and tied one around the neck of each bottle, and he tied each of the other ends to a crossbeam in the living room. He brought a hammer and said to his friends, "Here is a hammer. If you hit a bottle with the hammer and no water spills out, then you have attained Buddha's mind. Let's try this."

These monks were very proud. Not trying would look bad, but if they tried, they might fail. They decided to try.

First, the monk who did strong mantra practice hit the bottle. All the water came splashing down. Then the sutra monk hit the bottle with the hammer, and again all the water splashed out.

Finally, it was Bu Sol Go Sa's turn. He didn't use a hammer. He only pointed to the bottle and shouted KATZ! This katz was as loud as a cannon blast. The two monks leapt up in surprise as the bottle shattered and fell to the floor, but the water only spun around and around and did not come down.

Then the monks fell to the ground, bowed to him, and said, "We are sorry! Please teach us!"

He smiled and said, "I cannot teach you. You already have everything. But you must find your true selves; then you can do anything."

Then he took the bottle-shaped water and spilled it out the door.

This is the story of Bu Sol Go Sa.

When you are sick, only be sick. Then you will get everything, and you will be able to do anything.

You already said that this sickness is very strong teaching for you. That is wonderful. So I ask you: your sickness and Bu Sol Go Sa's sickness—are they the same or different? If you say the same, you can see the stars when your eyes are closed. If you say different, you are already in a dark hell with no door. What can you do?

Yours in the Dharma,
S. S.

A HOUSE ON FIRE

Berkeley, California
July 22, 1977

Dear Soen Sa Nim,

It is Friday afternoon and I have just seen three clients in a row in psychotherapy who feel totally "stuck." All three have created their lives so they can see no way out of their situations. *So much suffering!* Since I have been studying Buddhism, I understand better the causes of that suffering—desire, anger, and ignorance—but helping other people to understand and to *decide* to do something about it is another matter. Hitting pillows and "getting out the feelings" are not enough. More Kwan Seum Bosals!

Ezra and I are thinking of you.

> All our love,
> Diana

July 26, 1977

Dear Diana,

How are you and Ezra and your family? Thank you for your letter.

You said that some clients visited you and that they were suffering very much. Buddha said that this world is like a house on fire. He said that it is an ocean of suffering. Let's look at these words.

Many people get some things and don't get other things. But getting and not getting are the same. If they don't get something, they suffer; if they do get something, it will eventually disappear so they will suffer.

For example, suppose you had a dream last night and you are very attached to that dream, carrying it with you all through the day. When you were dreaming, you did not think the dream was good or bad—you were just dreaming. But later, if you like the dream, you want to carry it with you and if you don't like the dream, you want to forget it. But a dream is a dream. If you want to hold onto it or push it away, you have a problem; this is the appearance of likes and dislikes. Many people don't understand that likes and dislikes are also a dream. A sleeping dream and everyday thinking are both dreams; they do not exist. If you understand this non-existence, then you will understand that keeping is not necessary, and pushing away is not necessary. Put it all down!

Here is another example of suffering. Suppose there is a small jar full of candy. If you put your hand into the jar and grab a handful of candy, you cannot get your hand out. There will be much suffering: "Ahh—I can't get my hand out!" If you put down the mind that wants the candy, then you can get your hand out, and there is no suffering. You can't get your hand out? Why? Who made this suffering? If you put down your desire and your thinking, then your hand will slip out easily. There's no problem at all.

You said, "Hitting pillows and 'getting out the feelings' are not enough." You are right. These actions only change feelings—they do not help a person to understand karma, or cause and effect. You said "More Kwan Seum Bosals!" This is correct. Kwan Seum Bosal will make bad karma disappear. Then, if you put it all down, anything is possible. Many people want peace and happiness. Buddha said, "If you keep Bodhi mind moment to moment, you will get happiness everywhere."

Great Bodhisattva action means acting with great love and great sadness. So when someone is suffering, you are suffering. How can you teach them? When someone who is suffering a lot visits you, if you become one mind with them and speak about these things, this is great Bodhisattva action; this is Kwan Seum Bosal.

I hope you always go straight—Kwan Seum Bosal, and become Kwan Seum Bosal, soon finish the great work of life and death, and save all beings from suffering.

Yours in the Dharma,
S. S.

TIME TO MOVE FROM
THE CENTER OF THE ROOF

Cambridge, Massachusetts
February 22, 1978

Dear Soen Sa Nim,

Though I have spoken with you before and taken the Five Precepts, I wanted to write to you to introduce myself and ask formally to be one of your students. I have been attending Dharma talks and Yong Maeng Jong Jins at the Cambridge Zen Center for ten months. I sit Zen for an hour at home every morning and sometimes for an hour in the evening. I would like to describe how I became interested in your teaching and then ask a question.

One day, when I was very young, some friends and I decided to climb the roof of a large barn nearby. It was very steep and high, and we decided to go out from the inside of the barn through a second-story window. When my turn came, without really thinking about what I was doing, I climbed out the window and started up the roof. There was no problem; it was easy and fun. When I got about halfway up, I suddenly looked down, realized where I was, and was filled with fear. I stopped. I couldn't move. I lay there and just tried to hold on. I couldn't go up, and I couldn't go back down. I stayed that way for a long time. Finally, with my father offering words of encouragement from the ground, I fearfully inched my way back down to the window, and safety.

During my youth I was to many people an ideal child. I worked very hard in school and got good grades, and constantly went out of my way to please people with my actions.

I never thought about what I was doing. I simply went along with what others expected of me.

When I was fifteen, my world came crashing down. I began to doubt what I was doing in my life. I stopped trying in school and started to shy away from people.

Everyone seemed selfish, including myself; everyone, it seemed, only thought of himself. I wondered what the point was in trying. The things we were taught to work for—success and victory over others—somehow didn't feel right. I wondered what the purpose of life was, what goal was the right one to work towards.

The more confused I became and the less I tried, the worse it got. I learned what it felt like for people to disapprove of you, to scare you about the consequences of not doing what you're supposed to, what it felt like when they considered you strange and mentally sick. It was like a circle: the more confused I got, the more others doubted and questioned me, making me even more afraid of them and their ways.

Gradually, it got better, and I stopped questioning so much and simply went along with how things were. In college, I started out intending to be a doctor, not because I gave it much thought but because it was a praiseworthy profession. One year I was there, I decided to study very hard to see if I could succeed and achieve very high grades. I did, but when I did, the achievement felt very empty.

After college, I "dropped out." I didn't believe in anything and didn't know what to believe in. I've spent the years since then out of control, as if adrift on a raft at sea, trying desperately to hold on while being battered and tossed about by whatever waves came along. I've been drifting aimlessly and helplessly, without a goal. I've been unable to commit myself to any situation in life, including jobs, marriage, and place to live. I haven't been able even to commit myself to my wife, family, and friends.

I feel like I'm halfway up the roof again, unable to move, just trying to hold on. I want very much to learn what my correct job is and to be able to help other people. I would like to write popular songs and other types of music, but I'm afraid that my reasons for wanting to are selfish. Is this a good way to help people, or should I only do Zen? I think it's time to move away from the center of the roof.

Thank you very much for your teaching.

Sincerely yours,
Steve

March 4, 1978

Dear Steve,

How are you? Thank you for your letter.

Now I understand your situation and your mind. I had an experience in my childhood similar to yours when you were a child. In Korea, people use grass cuttings to make compost. Cutting the grass with a sickle was a job for children. When I was eight years old I liked the job, so one day my friends and I went out and I cut a lot of grass. Then we gathered it all in a bag, and we all went to school together. On the way, one of my friends said to me, "You cut your leg!" Then I looked at my leg and saw the blood. I was bleeding very badly, and the blood was making squishing sounds in my rubber shoe as I walked. As soon as I saw this, I fell to the ground in great pain and couldn't move. The other students all came around to see what had happened, and they ran to get my mother and helped me to the hospital.

I had already walked half a mile with no feeling—very happy. Then I saw my leg. So I had a problem, not because of the cut, but because I checked something and held that feeling. Before checking is called go-straight mind—there is no problem. After checking, then feelings, I-my-me, and problems appear. After I looked at my leg I had great pain, but not before! So I fell down and couldn't move. When you went out onto the roof, you had go-straight mind. Then, you checked something so you couldn't move and were afraid—"How can I get down?"

If we look at this life, we see it is the same. We see that nobody guarantees it. Everything in our life is very dangerous: it doesn't exist; it is illusion. If you see this, you cannot move. Everything has name and form, but name and form are empty. If you attain this, there is no name, no form.

If you attain no name and no form, then you will see that name is only name, and form is only form. Attaining no name and no form means your mind mirror is clean and not-moving. Then many colors can come and go with no problem.

So if you are holding something, if you make something, if you are attached to something, then your mind-mirror is dirty and it doesn't reflect clearly. If your mind is clear, there is nothing in it; everything is reflected. When red comes, red; when white comes, white. If somebody is sad, I am sad: if somebody is happy, I am happy. This mind is complete freedom, no hindrance. So you must put down I-my-me and don't make anything, don't hold anything, don't attach to anything. Only go straight—don't know. This don't-know mind will fix any sickness you have.   You want to save all people from suffering. This is possible. Don't-know mind is great love, great compassion, great Bodhisattva mind. Already, you have this direction. But if you want to help other people, you must be able to control your karma. Practicing by yourself is not good, not bad, but sometimes your karma appears and you cannot control your thinking and your actions. Then you cannot keep the correct way, and practicing Zen moment to moment is not possible. To learn to control your karma, action with other people is very important. At the Zen Center people live together and practice bowing, chanting, and sitting. If you try this, you won't hold your idea, your situation, and your condition; your I-my-me karma will disappear. So only go straight— don't know, and come live at a Zen Center, O.K.? Then your karma will become clear.

Clear karma means correct opinion, correct condition, correct situation, and moment-to-moment Bodhisattva mind. For you, if correct karma means that you like music, then try music. Then your music will save all beings. I hope you only go straight—don't know, make clear karma, get Enlightenment, and save all beings from suffering.

Yours in the Dharma,
S. S.

V. FORMS OF ZEN PRACTICE

WHAT IS STRONG SITTING?

Toronto, Canada
January 29, 1977

Dear Soen Sa Nim,

I miss you very much and wish that I did not live so far away from you. Every day I sit Zen and bow 108 times—Lawlor and I do this together. But often when I'm bowing and sitting, I am thinking: "What will I make for dinner? What shall I wear to work? Thinking is no good." All thinking!

You say—"Put it all down. Only go straight." But isn't there some balance about practice? Maybe I should do more sitting. You talk about strong sitting. What is this?

What am I? I ask this more and more through my day. But there is so much thinking!

I hope you are well, and I send you my great love.

Sherry

February 22, 1977

Dear Sherry,

How are you? Thank you for your letter.

You told me that you and Lawlor have been practicing together every day—that is wonderful. A lot of thinking, no thinking, a little thinking—it doesn't matter. You say, "thinking is no good." *This* is no good. This is being attached to your thinking. Only try, try, try, and your thinking will rest. Then finally, at bowing time, only bow; at sitting time, only sit; at chanting time, only chant. This is possible. If you keep practicing, this will happen.

In your letter you asked me about balance in your practice and about strong sitting. If you are attached to something, your mind and your body will be unbalanced. If you don't make anything, your mind and your body become one, and so they will be perfectly balanced, and everything will be complete and clear.

Strong sitting means not checking your mind and feelings. At times everyone has many thoughts and feelings while sitting. This is correct. Don't worry. But many people check themselves. "I am no good. What do other people think of me? I am always thinking. How can I cut off all thinking? How do you only go straight? How do you put it all down?" This is being attached to thinking. Thinking itself is not bad or good. Just don't be attached to thinking. Don't worry about everything. Thinking is thinking; feeling is feeling. Don't touch. Only go straight—don't know. That is strong sitting.

If you keep this strong-sitting mind, your mind will be clear moment to moment. Clear mind means keeping your correct situation. When you drive, just drive. Then when you come to a red light, stop. When it turns green, go. That is the correct situation. Correct situation means just-like-this.

I understand your mind. Your mind constantly checks your mind. But if you practice and try every day, your checking mind will rest, and you will be able to keep a just-like-this mind. Then when you see the sky, only blue; when you see a tree, only green. Your mind is still. Then saving all beings is possible.

I hope you only go straight—don't know, keep a mind which is clear like space, attain Enlightenment, and save all beings from suffering.

Yours in the Dharma,
S. S.

AT SITTING TIME, ONLY SIT

Milwaukee, Wisconsin
March 15, 1977

Dear Soen Sa Nim,

I am one of the students who attended the sitting retreat in Chicago a few months ago. A week after I came home from Chicago, the discipline and training became difficult to maintain. I've always known that I am the type of student who needs group support or at least contact with a teacher every so often to reinforce and aid me to strengthen my training. I am a low-class Zen student! If you could answer a few questions I may be able to strengthen my practice.

First, I must tell you I'm a beginner in Zen practice. You told me when I sit to breathe in three counts, "Clear mind," and exhale seven counts, "Don't know."

Questions: What should I do if I'm having difficulty centering my focus and energy in the *hara*? Instead of just sitting, I am thinking "What should I be doing?" and therefore I am not sitting. At the last interview I had during the Chicago Yong Maeng Jong Jin, you gave me a kong-an, Hyang Eom's "Up a Tree" ("Mind Meal," Fifth Gate). My answer: "Let him down from the tree!" When I sit, do I breathe the three and the seven counts, or do I concentrate on the kong-an?

Soen Sa Nim, something is deeply concerning me. I feel very free, but I'm afraid that this overwhelming feeling of freedom can in some way confine me. I am attached to being free and am also thinking that this free feeling is very radical and is not really the basis for any type of spiritual growth.

Is it true that there is really no "right" or "wrong" behavior? If this is the way it is, then it doesn't matter if I go out and commit murder or become a thief. If I am free, I am not attached to anything; it doesn't matter what I do. I'm afraid of falling into some delusion or Zen sickness. Can you straighten me out on this point of freedom?

Let me give you an example. A person could go out and hurt many people—what is to stop this person? Hurt is created by thinking mind, so there isn't really any hurt; it doesn't matter what one does to others! It really doesn't matter if I train in Zen practice either. If I sit and train, then I am attached to sitting.

I deeply thank you for stopping in Chicago and sharing your wisdom with us. Please, visit again! May you continue to teach.

Thanks!
Dusanka

April 1, 1977

Dear Dusanka,

Thank you for your letter. How are you? You say it is difficult to practice by yourself. Also you say you are a low-class Zen student. I ask you, what are you? Where are you coming from? What is your name? How old are you? You already understand that 10,000 questions return to one question, What am I? Don't know! What is don't-know? Tell me! Very simple. Don't make anything. Only go straight—don't know. O.K.?

Next, at sitting time, only sit. Don't make *Hara*, don't make energy, don't make kong-an, don't make anything. Breathe in for three counts, "Clear mind, clear mind, clear mind." Then for seven counts breathe out, "*Don't-know.*"

In your kong-an answer, if you open your mouth, you are already dead! Don't keep the kong-an in your head. You must only go straight—don't know. This is very important. It is like this: when a mother sends her son to war, even though she works, eats, talks to her friends, and watches television, she always keeps in her mind the question, "When will my son come home?" Keeping don't-know mind is the same as this. So you must only go straight—don't know in your everyday life, not only when you are sitting. Then when it is time to answer a kong-an, an answer will appear.

You write about freedom. This is *thinking* freedom. You must *attain* freedom. Your idea of freedom has no direction. Why do you want freedom? What is the purpose of freedom? Let your mind go any place without hindrance; then you will understand correct freedom. If you completely attain freedom, there is no life, no death. The mind that attains freedom is clear like space. How do you attain this? And how do you use freedom?

You talk about someone killing somebody or hurting other people, so I say to you, don't make I-my-me. What is the purpose of your life? You say, "I," "I," "I," "I," "I." What kind of I is this? You must *kill* this I. Then there will be no I. When there is no I, your mind will be clear like space. Then you are free! If you become free, you will get everything. Keeping clear-like-space mind, moment to moment, means your mind is like a clear mirror. When red comes, red; when white comes, white.

Then how do you use freedom from life and death? Clear-like-space mind is Bodhisattva mind. If somebody is sad, I am sad; if somebody is happy, I am happy. Then there is no inside, no outside; inside and outside become one. Then good and bad appear by themselves, and you must use everything to help other people. This is great love and the great Bodhisattva way.

I hope you always keep don't-know, then get Enlightenment and true freedom, and save all beings from suffering.

Yours in the Dharma,
S. S.

LOST MIND, ONE MIND, CLEAR MIND

Forest Knolls, California
July 28, 1977

Dear Soen Sa Nim,

Hello, how are you?

I came to the Dharma Talk you gave at the Berkeley Empty Gate Zen Center during your last visit. I thought then that I would sit the three-day Yong Maeng Jong Jin when you come West next time, but I have an obligation that weekend, so I decided to try the three-day chanting retreat, the Kido, instead.

I understand that if I sit and keep a don't-know mind I might experience a clear, just-now view of things. But I don't see how that happens if you chant for a long time. I think I might miss the point so I wonder if you could tell me a little about chanting before the Kido so I will know how to try.

Thanks for your time. I look forward to seeing you in September.

Love,
Bonnie

August 10, 1977

Dear Bonnie,

How are you? Thank you for your letter.

You came to the Empty Gate Zen Center and you decided to try the Kido next month. That is wonderful—chanting is very good practice.

During the Kido we will chant "Kwan Seum Bosal, Kwan Seum Bosal" ten hours a day for three days. When you first try chanting, you won't understand how to use chanting to keep a clear mind. Sometimes your mouth is doing Kwan Seum Bosal, but your mind is at home, in San Francisco, or in New

York. But then, "No good, come back!" says your thinking.

In Buddhism there is a theory about eight kinds of consciousness. The first six are related to your senses—your eyes, ears, nose, tongue, body, and mind. Chanting the words "Kwan Seum Bosal" is the action of your sixth consciousness; going to San Francisco or New York is the action of your eighth consciousness; "Come back!" is your seventh consciousness in action. Your sixth consciousness controls your body. Your seventh consciousness is your discriminating consciousness: "I like this; I don't like that." Or, "Do this; don't do that." Your eighth consciousness is your memory or storehouse consciousness. If you want to keep one mind, then the seventh consciousness talks to the eighth consciousness: "Come back!" But if these three consciousnesses are acting separately, you are not chanting correctly. This is lost mind.

As you continue with chanting practice, you will experience one-mind chanting. You don't hear the sound; you go into the sound—you and the sound become one. Only Kwan Seum Bosal, Kwan Seum Bosal, Kwan Seum Bosal. This is Kwan Seum Bosal samadhi—only one mind.

The Heart Sutra says, "Avalokitesvara Bodhisattva perceives that all five skandhas are empty." This means that form, feelings, perceptions, impulses, and consciousness all are empty. Your consciousness is empty, so your sixth, seventh, and eighth consciousnesses are completely empty. If you keep this mind, then your eyes, ears, nose, tongue, body, and mind are all empty. The Heart Sutra says, "No eyes, no ears, no nose, no tongue, no body, no mind, no realm of eyes and so forth until no object of mind." Then your mind is no mind. No mind means no feeling, no Buddha, no God, nothing at all. So your mind is clear like space. Then you can hear your voice; you can hear all the sounds very clearly; your mind is clear like space. You perceive all sounds just as they are. This is clear mind.

One mind is not-moving, empty mind; clear mind is using this mind meticulously moment to moment. One mind is like pushing "clear" on your calculator; clear mind means using your calculator: $1 + 2 = 3$.

Kwan Seum Bosal is very important. *Kwan* means perceive; *se* means world; *um* means sound; *Bosal* means Bodhisattva. You must perceive world sound. You must perceive the sound of your voice. This is clear mind.

Then the world sound and your sound, are they are the same or different? At that time, the sound is no sound: form is emptiness; emptiness is form. But when there is no sound, there is no I, no Buddha, no God, so there is no form, no emptiness—nothing at all. If there is nothing at all, then your mind is clear. Then your true self is very clear like a clear mirror.

Then form is form; emptiness is emptiness. So color is color; sound is sound. When you see the sky, only blue; when you see a tree, only green. During the Kido, when you hear, there is only the sound of the *moktak*, the sound of the drums, the sound of chanting voices.

So during the Kido I hope you only go straight—Kwan Seum Bosal. Perceive world sound. This is your true self. Then you can hear everything clearly, perceive everything clearly, and use this Kwan Seum Bosal mind to become a great Bodhisattva and save all beings from suffering.

Yours in the Dharma,
S. S.

LOW-CLASS PRACTICE

Allston, Massachusetts
September 14, 1977

Dear Soen Sa Nim,

How are you? I hope you are well, even though you are

working so hard. Everyone at the Cambridge Zen Center says hello to you and to our West Coast family.

I must tell you something. This summer, I came to believe in Buddhism 100%, so I am very happy. Before, there was a lot of fighting in my mind about whether or not to practice. But this summer, a lot of bad karma disappeared. This fighting stopped, so practicing became possible. Also, I was able to quit smoking—something I thought I'd never be able to do in a million years. How did this happen?

Do you remember two years ago when a lot of bad karma appeared in my mind, and I moved out of the Zen Center and stopped practicing? Then you gave me the mantra: "*Gate, gate, paragate, parasamgate, bodhi svaha.*" Within three months I was back at the Zen Center, practicing. Then you said, "O.K., your mind is stronger, so now you must breathe in, 'Clear mind,' and breathe out, 'Don't know.'" I did this practice for a while, even though I did not like it. But, at the beginning of the summer, my old bad karma again appeared —"I hate Zen; I don't want to practice." So I started doing the mantra again. And again, this bad karma disappeared.

Now, I don't understand mantras. All I know is that when I begin to lose my direction, this mantra sets me straight again. Is it O.K. to do it all the time—even when my mind is strong? Some people say that using a mantra is a very low-class practice. Is this true? Please tell me about using a mantra.

Thank you for teaching me about Buddhism.

Love,
Dyan

September 21, 1977

Dear Dyan,

Thank you for your letter. How are you? The West Coast family says hello to you and the Cambridge Zen Center family.

You say that you believe in Buddhism 100%. I am glad to hear that! Congratulations on your practice becoming very strong. You also said that you stopped smoking; that is wonderful.

In your letter, you wrote about mantra and don't-know mind. Some people say that using a mantra is low-class. That is wrong. It is their thinking that is low-class. The *Compass of Zen Teaching* says, "Without thinking, sutra practice, mantra practice, *yom bul* (repeating the Buddha's name) practice, and Zen practice are all the same, but if you are attached to thinking and attached to words, all practices are different." When we eat, some people use chopsticks, some use forks, some use spoons, some use fingers. What you use is not important—did you get a full stomach? Whether you use a mantra or kong-ans is not important. What matters is how you keep just-now mind moment to moment. If you understand this, you can always keep enough-mind.

That is the Great Vow, not only in this lifetime but for numberless lifetimes to come—to save other people.

You already have the mantra, "*Gate, gate paragate, parasamgate, bodhi svaha!*" You have very good karma with this mantra, so use this good karma for all beings. Don't check your mind; don't check your feelings; don't check other people's minds. Only go straight—don't know with your mantra—then, no problem.

Many people want to climb to the top of a mountain. One person begins to climb from the south side of the mountain; someone else begins from the north side, another from the west side, and another from the east side. They only go straight and arrive at the top, but the person on the south side thinks the direction of the person on the north side is wrong. Each thinks the others' directions are wrong. Don't check another's direction; this is no good. All arrive at the top, at the same point; that is most important.

There is one important point about mantra practice you

must understand. With mantra, getting one mind and samadhi are very easy. But you cannot find your True Way if you are attached to mantra. Mantra alone has no direction. However, "Who is doing the mantra?" means having a direction. Having a direction means keeping a question and letting your cognition become clear so you can perceive your correct situation.

So only mantra is one mind, but if you keep the great question and mantra, that is clear mind.

Only-go-straight don't-know mind is clear like space. There is no subject, no object, no inside, no outside. When you are doing something, you must do it. If you are not thinking, that is correct mantra and correct don't-know mind. What does the cat say? What does the dog say? You already understand.

I hope you only go straight—don't-know with your mantra, soon become a great Bodhisattva, finish the Great Work of life and death, get Enlightenment, and save all beings from suffering.

Yours in the Dharma,
S. S.

CORRESPONDENCE WITH DIANA

Berkeley, California
July 29, 1976

Dear Soen Sa Nim,

I am trying very hard to keep Kwan Seum Bosal in my mind, since more than anything I would like to do whatever it takes to walk the Bodhisattva path.

I have started many letters to you in the past week but they have all ended up in the wastebasket. These wastebasket letters mainly explained my problems and obstacles with my practice. Yet, since the problems and obstacles keep changing, it must be that this is an important part of the process for me— to face my restlessness, boredom, anger, judgmentalness, and not get attached to them. I am sure you are aware that people experience such things when they sit or do Kwan Seum Bosal or whatever!

I found your book, *Dropping Ashes on the Buddha*, in the store yesterday, and from the quick leafing through I've had time for, it looks great! One question: I read the chapter on your life—why is it necessary to do such harsh things to our bodies to become Enlightened? I can see accepting the suffering that comes of itself in life, but why inflict it on ourselves?

Kwan Seum Bosal. And much love.

Diana

August 10, 1976

Dear Diana,

How are you? Thank you for your letter.

You say trying to keep Kwan Seum Bosal in your mind every day is very difficult. If you chant slowly, thinking appears; if you chant quickly, thinking is not possible. Then you can make new karma. Then, whether you are sitting, talking, watching television, or playing golf, in your mind there will be only KwanSeumBosalKwanSeumBosalKwanSeumBosal. Then Kwan Seum Bosal is sitting, talking, watching television, or playing golf. Only don't-know. This is correct practicing.

You said that you face your restlessness, boredom, anger and judgmentalness. This means that it is possible to change your life. Finally you will realize that this life is a dream. What is correct life? Correct life is beyond time and space. Then there is no life, no death. You will get freedom from life and death—complete freedom.

You asked me why the body must suffer. When I went on retreat, I was very young and very strong, so I had many desires.

Sometimes I was very angry—very angry at other people and at the whole world. Also, sometimes ignorance appeared. I looked at these three things—desire, anger, and ignorance—and asked where they came from. They come from our bodies. If you can completely control your body, then you can completely control your desire, anger and ignorance.

All Buddhas have tried difficult practices. When these three things—desire, anger and ignorance—appear, our minds become dark. After hard practice, these three things disappear. After my retreat, my mind was bright and clear like space. You must try a retreat sometime; then you will understand why hard training is important.

Here is a new kong-an for you.

Soeng Am Calls Master ("Mind Meal," Third Gate)

Master Soeng Am Eon used to call himself every day, "Master!" and would answer, "Yes?"

"You must keep clear!"

"Yes!"

"Never be deceived by others, any day, any time!"

"Yes! Yes!"

Soeng Am Eon used to call himself and answer himself, two minds. Which one is the correct Master?

I hope you always go straight—don't know, soon find a good answer to your homework, get Enlightenment, and save all beings from suffering.

Yours in the Dharma,
S. S.

P.S. I am sending you some pictures and a tape from the Kido.

August 18, 1976

Dear Soen Sa Nim,

I returned last Friday from twelve days of "hard sitting" at a Vipassana meditation retreat led by Jack Kornfield, whom you know. There was your letter and Kido tape and pictures to welcome me home! Thank you so much! Although all that sitting was "good" for me, what a gift to hear you chanting! I have missed the bowing and chanting ceremony, and the sound of your bell.

This retreat was the first time in years I have been away from my family and my usual life. Very strange. We lived very simply: a place far off in the country, no electricity, everything slowed way down, no talking, a mother banty hen and eleven baby chicks, a full moon, hot mineral springs for our sore muscles, and good teaching from Jack. Nevertheless, it was the hardest thing I've ever done—facing my many attachments.

While there, I found the answer to the question I asked you: why it is necessary to make our bodies suffer. It just is, that's all! The axle, the wheels need breaking for the mind to be still. I feel discouraged about this ever happening to me; yet I think that I scare myself when I look at the huge mountains of my ego, my habits, the way my small "I" is.

I am trying to take each minute as a chance to let go to Big "I." Bowing is still the easiest way for me to do that. Better than Kwan Seum Bosal—I can now do three thousand in thirty to forty minutes, fast like you said, but all I end up with is a headache! To each his own! When I run in the mornings, for exercise, I like to keep rhythm with Kwan Seum Bosal—it keeps me in the here and now, not-thinking thinking. Also, when I'm listening to my clients (I have a small private practice as a psychotherapist), the Kwan Seum Bosal often pops into my mind and helps me pay attention to the person and not just their words.

Words are such a terrible way of communicating, and yet how can people know each other without them? Especially at a distance?

We are both very eager to be a part of what you are doing—"to save all beings from suffering." What else is important?

Love,
Diana

Dear Diana,

Thank you very much for your letter. How are you and Ezra?

You said you sat for twelve days' hard training. That is wonderful. Hard training is like dry-cleaning the mind. People use their minds every day, but they do not clean their minds, so their minds get dirty. Then bad karma appears and it is even more difficult to become clear. So hard training is very important.

You said you were practicing with Jack. Jack is a very good teacher. And you understand about making our bodies suffer: "It just is." That is wonderful. This intuition comes from clear mind. Intuition means no subject, no object—inside and outside become one. If you keep this mind always, moment to moment, you can understand your correct opinion, your correct condition, your correct situation.

Most people separate their opinion, their condition, and their situation, but if you have a clear mind, your opinion, condition, and situation become one action—you cannot separate them. When you are working, only work; when you return home, only keep a mother's mind; when talking to your husband, only keep a wife's mind; when driving, only drive; when walking, only walk; when eating, only eat. Correct action moment to moment is your correct opinion, correct situation, and correct condition. Don't check anything. Only go straight—Kwan Sum Bosal. Then you will get everything.

You want your small I to disappear and to become big I. This is just your thinking: put it down. Also when you are sitting and doing Kwan Seum Bosal, you are attached to Kwan Seum Bosal, so you get a headache. When you are outside, walking around, and you try Kwan Seum Bosal, you don't get a headache. Don't be attached to Kwan Seum Bosal—only try. Then soon you will be able to use Kwan Seum Bosal to keep a clear mind.

You said words are a terrible way of communicating. But words are important. If you are attached to words, your words will control you. So you must control your words. This means that your words and speech do not hinder your true self. If you are thinking, you are limited by your words. That is why we practice Zen. If you are not thinking, you have freedom from your words and so there is no problem.

How is your homework? You must soon find Seong Am's master and tell me! I hope you only go straight—don't know, find your true master, get Enlightenment, and save all beings from suffering.

Yours in the Dharma,
S. S.

UNDERSTAND YOUR SICKNESS, THEN TAKE THE CORRECT MEDICINE

Vancouver, Canada
August 8, 1977

Dear Soen Sa Nim,

Thank you very much for the "very special long time in coming" Precepts Ceremony.

Several days ago, I was having lunch with a friend of mine who asked me about Zen practice, and I tried very hard to give her some insights. I once tried some ketamine, and my experience of this was flowing through a blaze of soft colors—I *was* and knew the questions and answers; I became the truth. It was this strange paradox of flowing that I tried to explain and to equate to Zen, but the words were not sufficient without the experience. You mentioned that sometimes during a retreat it is possible to "see your karma." When you have seen this, do you stop the flow, or simply keep "don't-know mind"? Like breathing and thinking during meditation, we watch our thoughts without stopping them—is it the same with "seeing your karma"?

You say during meditation, "only go straight clear mind—don't know"; then you say, "you must try, try, try." Some say, "you must surrender," and that to "try" is too North American and individualistic, flowing against the current of the stream.

Thank you for your wonderful "clear mind—don't know."

Matthew

August 16, 1977

Dear Matthew,

Thank you for your letter. How are you? You liked the Precepts Ceremony. That is wonderful. In a previous lifetime you made karma, so you are getting the result in this lifetime. I think you have karma which is rare: you have strong Buddhist karma. This special karma revolves through primary cause, dependent origination, and result, making great love, great compassion, and great Bodhisattva action. How wonderful it is!

You say you took ketamine and experienced being the truth. Just now, what are you doing? If you attain truth, moment to moment you can see; you can hear—everything is truth.

If you cannot attain truth, then what you say is truth is not truth. It is your thinking-truth. Your thinking-truth is illusion. So you must be *very* careful. Ketamine mind and Zen mind are different. Ketamine mind is losing your mind; Zen mind is clear mind.

Losing your mind means losing your true self. You cannot find your true self if you think, "color is truth." Your thinking makes "color is truth." Where does color come from? Color does not exist. In the samsara of name and form, something changes and becomes color. Color is empty. So your truth is empty. So if you are attached to color, already you have lost your true self. We say, "the dog runs away with the bone."

Clear mind means when color comes, then color; color goes, then color goes. Clear mind means attaining your true self. If you are not attached to color, then you will find your true self.

LSD and ketamine help some people. Some people are very attached to name and form, so these special medicines give an experience of emptiness, and then cutting attachment is very easy. But you cannot *attain* truth this way. To attain truth, you must *practice* the correct way. Many people are attached to good feelings so they take more and more and more medicine. This is very dangerous. An eminent teacher said, "People with mirage-sickness use mirage-medicine. When the sickness is gone, throw away the mirage-medicine. Then you will return to what is originally human."

Many people are very attached to name and form. That is mirage-sickness. Mirage-medicine is ketamine or LSD or marijuana. But if your mirage-sickness goes away, you must throw away these medicines. This is very necessary. If you don't throw away these medicines you will get mirage-medicine-sickness. That is very dangerous. If you are attached to these medicines, you lose your true way.

You asked about your karma appearing on a retreat.

Your karma appears not only on retreat; it also appears when you take special medicine. Also if you do hard practicing, then anytime, anywhere, your karma appears. But don't worry about your karma. Only go straight—don't touch your karma. So I say to you, understanding your karma means only understanding: don't touch.

Practicing means you must perceive your karma. As you practice more strongly you will perceive that your karma is made by your thinking. If you cut off all thinking, you can see that originally your karma is empty. We call this attaining primary point. Seeing this, it is possible to develop a mind that does not attach to anything. This means that you are no longer attached to your karma; your karma does not control you. Then you can see; you can hear; just-like-this is truth. Then you can use your karma clearly and correctly to save all people from suffering. So karma coming and going, color coming and going, doesn't matter. Only go straight—don't make anything. Then your karma will become clear, no hindrance, and you can use your karma to help other people.

You say "try" and "surrender." If you are attached to words, you don't understand the meaning of "try" and the meaning of "surrender." Again I say: only go straight—don't know. Sometimes "try, try, try"; sometimes "don't make anything"; sometimes "put it all down"; sometimes "don't make anything." These are only teaching words. These teaching words only show direction; they have no meaning. Many people have word-sickness, so these words are word-medicine. If you are attached to words, you have already made a mistake. If you are not attached to words, then try, surrender, put it all down, only go straight, keep clear mind are all the same. But if you say the same, I hit you. If you say different, I will also hit you. What can you do? You already understand. So I say to you, only go straight—don't know. Try, try, try.

You must finish your kong-an homework. Sometime, you must eat your mind meal ("Mind Meal," Appendix I). There are ten gates. If you pass all ten gates, you can make anything—no hindrance. But if you haven't passed them yet, you must always take don't-know medicine. This medicine can digest all your karma and all your complicated headache sickness. Then your eyes, ears, nose, tongue, body, mind will become as clear as Buddha. Then, you are Buddha. What more do you want?

I hope you only go straight—don't know, then soon throw away don't-know, soon become great love don't-know, and great compassion don't-know, and great Bodhisattva don't-know, then save all beings from suffering.

Yours in the Dharma,
S. S.

VI. ON KONG-AN PRACTICE

WOOF WOOF, BETTER THAN
ZEN MASTER JO JU

Los Angeles, California
October 28, 1976

Dear Soen Sa Nim,

I wish to thank you for coming to the West Coast. Your teaching is always appreciated by many. When you come, I am always returned to the fundamental teachings: drop it, just straight ahead, and just-like-this. At the end of two months, I am back again to this point.

When you leave, I return to Kozan Roshi and visit other teachers and do lots of reading, since each of these other people emphasizes a complete familiarity with all Zen kong-ans and scriptures. Temporarily, confusion arises and a losing of the fundamental point. But even before you return from the East Coast, the confusion begins to disappear and when you come, it disappears even more. Each time this happens I have a new teaching that has been penetrated and dropped. This penetration and dropping allows me to become a better teacher for the type of people that come to my classes at U.C.L.A. since they are academic types and are attracted to people that "know."

Yet, I only teach about not knowing, and use the knowing to end knowing.

When you come, it is like a hand opening, relaxing. When you leave, returning to traditional Zen practice is like hand closing, becoming tight. This closing, then opening, tensing and relaxing is good.

I hope that all the centers grow. It is very important that your understanding be transmitted to as many people as possible.

Thank you very much.

Sincerely,
Ed

Dear Ed,

How are you? Thank you for your letter. Your letter is not good, not bad, but you do not listen to me.

I always say, "Don't make anything; then you will get everything." But you make something all the time. Why make me? Why make Kozan Roshi? Why make other teachers? Why make reading books? If you don't make anything, then you will not be hindered by me, by Kozan Roshi, by other teachers, or by books. Also you will not lose the fundamental point.

I always worry about you. You are too clever; you follow your clever thinking. You say, "Yet, I only teach about not knowing and use this to end knowing." What does this mean? I hit you thirty times!

Don't use dead words. You are a Zen student! You must use live words. Dead words are always opposite-thinking words. Live words are just-like-this words. Just-like-this words have no subject, no object; inside and outside only become one.

This is why we use kong-an practice. Kong-ans are like fishing hooks. If your mind is not clear, the baited hook will drop into the pool of your mind, all your thinking will appear, and you will swallow the hook and be caught by your thinking. If you cut off all thinking and only go straight—don't know, then the hook drops into clear mind and comes out of clear mind. You will perceive the correct situation in the kong-an and not touch the fishing hook.

A monk once asked Zen Master Jo Ju, "Does a dog have Buddha-nature?" Jo Ju answered, ""Mu!" (No!) ("Mind Meal," First Gate).

This is very bad speech! Why? What is the meaning of "Mu?" If it means no, not yes, this makes opposites; opposites are only thinking. If it has no opposite, then it has no meaning, so it has no truth. Zen Master Jo Ju used this bad speech to give his students a big question. This is a Zen Master's job. Jo Ju was a very great Zen Master, and his bad speech is one of the most important kong-ans in Zen practice.

So you must not swallow Jo Ju's fishing hook. Does a dog have Buddha-nature? You must cut off all opposites thinking— Buddha-nature, no Buddha-nature—HIT, become one. What is a dog's correct situation? You must ask a dog, O.K.? What does a dog say?

I have given you "Mind Meal" for homework. Zen Master Jo Ju's "Mu!" kong-an is the first of the ten gates. Mind Meal tests your mind: do you go for the bait? If you check the ten gates, the ten kong-ans, does hungry mind, desire mind, not-enough-mind appear? If so, you must eat your Mind Meal. You must completely digest your understanding. Then finishing your Mind Meal is possible. Then you get enough-mind, no-hindrance mind, no I-my-me mind. Enough-mind does not go for the bait, so everything is clear and you can perceive any situation in your life and kong-an clearly, and save all beings.

So Zen Master Jo Ju's "Mu!" is a saving-all-beings answer. Zen Master Po De said, "If light comes, hit light. If dark comes, hit dark. If Buddha comes, hit Buddha." You must hit your checking mind, your dead-words thinking. Then you can use live words and finish your Mind Meal.

I hope you only go straight—don't know, soon finish your Mind Meal, get Enlightenment, and save all beings from suffering.

Yours in the Dharma,
S. S.

THE MEANING OF KONG-AN PRACTICE

London, England
January 9, 1978

Dear Soen Sa Nim,

My husband Richard and I are so looking forward to meeting you when you come here in the spring. It is a nice time to come to England. I am now trying to arrange some good meetings for you in Oxford and Cambridge as well as London.

Before you arrive, I would very much like to begin to communicate with you, so that we are not strangers and can make real contact right away. Your student, Stephen, has suggested that to start with, I should perhaps make a comment on the kong-an given to you by your teacher, Zen Master Ko Bong, "The mouse eats cat food, but the cat-bowl is broken." ("Mind Meal," Tenth Gate)*

The first part of the answer you gave Zen Master Ko Bong, "The sky is blue; the grass is green," seems to refer to one's state when one has settled into one's "true, immovable self." This is when reality is where I am, and the whole outer world is appearance and is no longer made up of the powerful separate entities we think we see when we ourselves are not real.

There are no barriers. Whatever the situation is, one can respond to it freely. In this state one really sees the truth of such statements as, "There is no spiritual knowledge that I must seek," for what spiritual knowledge can there possibly be in finding out that existence, just as it is, is Nirvana, or that form is void and void is form? This state has nothing to do

---

* The story of the dialogue between Soen Sa Nim and Zen Master Ko Bong appears in the Chapter, "The Story of Seung Sahn Soen-Sa," in *Dropping Ashes on the Buddha.*

with knowledge, because it is a state of becoming alive. Whereas the world was dead before because it was only there for my own use and had no meaning in itself, now it is of total significance, and everything is equally significant.

This state happened to me for the first time some years ago. It came out of the blue, when I knew nothing of Buddhism, and it lasted about three and a half days. I thought it would last forever and I was desolate when it went. That's what set me searching until I discovered Buddhism, and in particular, Zen. Since then, it has often come back briefly, but nowadays my need for it is less. Two or three years after that first time, I was introduced to Yasutani Roshi, who was visiting London, and I told him about it. Later I was told that he had lodged a certificate of satori in my name in Kyoto, but we did not keep in touch.

When the grass is green and the sky is blue all things are right, and there is nothing to attain. And yet Zen Master Ko Bong told you that you had a bit more to answer. It seemed to me, when I thought about it, that you had not thrown away language in your answer. When the grass is green, there is still something. And I think the naming is at fault.

It doesn't matter if I live from the ephemeral world of labels which I have built up in my mind—in fact, I must do so, because I am a human being—but what *does* matter is that I should realize that my named world is just that, a named world which is fundamentally a complete mystery. I should not confuse the label with reality by ever thinking that saying "The sky is blue" is capturing the whole thing. The sky *is* blue.

But to *say* it is blue and think that this is a total answer is near, but not near enough. For me a little while ago it was blue. Now it just is. So when you answered, "just like this," you explained it all. At least as far as my understanding goes.

With very best wishes,
Yours sincerely,
Anne

January 20, 1978

Dear Anne,

Thank you for your letter. How are you and your husband Richard? Stephen has told me about you; I think you are a wonderful student.

You talk about kong-ans. Kong-ans are not special. If you make something special, you have something special, but this "special" cannot help you. If you keep your correct situation moment to moment, the mouse kong-an and all the other 1,700 kong-ans are no problem.

You said many times that the sky is blue and the grass is green. That was my understanding before I finished the mouse kong-an. Not good, not bad. We say that is only like-this, not just-like-this. Just-like-this means keeping your correct situation moment to moment. When you are hungry, what? If you say, "the sky is blue; the grass is green," that is not enough. You must *eat*. That is the correct situation when you are hungry.

You said, "Just as it is, is Nirvana—that form is void and void is form. This state has nothing to do with knowledge, because it is a state of becoming alive." I hit you thirty times! If you open your mouth again, you lose your tongue! You only *explain* "just as it is." This is called understanding. Understanding cannot help you. You must *attain* "just as it is." You say, "When grass is green, there is still something." This means you are attached to something. Being attached to words and using words are different. Being attached to words means you have a hindrance. Using words is only for other people, in great love and great compassion. That is the great Bodhisattva way.

Here is an example: Let's say we have a bell. The question is, "Is this a bell or not?" If you say it is a bell, you are attached to name and form. If you say it is not a bell, you are attached to emptiness. What can you do?

Maybe you answer with silence. This is 180° on the Zen Circle. This is like a mute who has had a dream. Then maybe you answer by hitting the floor or yelling, "KATZ!" This is demonstrating 180° on the Zen Circle, but you haven't answered the question. You only understand one; you don't understand two.

Then maybe you say, "The sky is blue; the grass is green," or "The wall is white," or "The bell is yellow." Not good, not bad. All these things are true, so we call this kind of response a "like-this" answer. But does this answer the question? It is like scratching your right foot when your left foot itches.

Is this a bell or not? What is your relationship to the bell? Pick up the bell and ring it. Words are not necessary. This is just-like-this. No subject, no object—inside and outside become one. You perceive your correct situation and act accordingly.

You met Yasutani Roshi, and he sent his certificate of satori for you to Kyoto. That is wonderful.

I will give you a kong-an:

Duk Sahn Carrying His Bowls
("Mind Meal," Eighth Gate)

One day Duk Sahn came into the Dharma Room carrying his bowls. Seol Bong (Housemaster), said, "Old Master, the bell has not yet been rung and the drum has not yet been struck. Where are you going, carrying your bowls?"

Duk Sahn returned to the Master's room. Seol Bong told Am Du (Head Monk). Am Du said, "Great Master Duk Sahn does not understand the last word."

Duk Sahn heard this and sent for Am Du. "Do you not approve of me?" he demanded. Then Am Du whispered in the Master's ear. Duk Sahn was relieved.

Next day on the rostrum, making his Dharma Speech, Duk Sahn was really different from before. Am Du went to the front of the Dharma Room, laughed loudly, clapped his hands and said, "Great joy! the old Master has understood the last word! From now on, no one can check him."

If you understand this kong-an, you must tell me the answer.

Then you understand just-like-this and the mouse kong-an. If you do not understand this kong-an, then you do not understand just-like-this and the mouse kong-an. Only go straight—don't know.

Don't check your understanding; don't check anything. A good answer, a bad answer, or no answer—this doesn't matter. How much do you believe in yourself? That is very important. If you believe in yourself 100%, all that you see and hear, all that you smell, taste and touch is the truth just as it is. That is a living, true kong-an. So I hope you only go straight—don't know, believe in yourself 100%, become a great Bodhisattva, and save all beings from suffering.

Yours in the Dharma,
S. S.

HEAD OF A DRAGON,
TAIL OF A SNAKE

Western Pennsylvania
November 1, 1977

Dear Soen Sa Nim,

How are you? In your last letter you asked me again, "Why does Bodhidharma have no beard?" ("Mind Meal," Fourth Gate). You said I must find a picture of Bodidharma to see that in pictures of him he always has a beard. In my last letter, I gave you a 90% answer, and the kong-an bomb did not explode. O.K.

Why does Bodhidharma have no beard?

Beard.

This is a feeble shot in the dark, of course, but I hope to be emptied of answers soon. I have not been able to put all of the time and effort into your kong-an that I previously intended, due to the fact that I have been using much of my free time to study electronics in the hopes of getting a good job. I have appreciated my electronics study as a Zen discipline, however, and am mastering it with a single-minded zeal and directness. Yet within me there is a need to get back to the kong-an and settle this matter. I wish to give all sentient beings the aid that only a Patriarch can give.

Too many words! Linda and I shall be very glad to hear from you again. Please take care of yourself and all beings.

Yours in the Dharma,
Dale

November 10, 1977

Dear Dale,

Thank you for your letter. How are you and Linda?

Your letter had much energy, but your kong-an answer has no energy. What's the matter with you? You must believe in yourself 100%! What are you doing now? When you do something, you must *do* it. That is your correct situation; that is clear mind; that is don't-know. You think that the kong-an is separate from your life and from your job. This kong-an, don't-know mind, clear mind, your job, your life—everything: Hit! become one. Just now, what are you doing?

You said, "I have no time, so I can't work on the kong-an." This is a very bad speech! Every kong-an points to its own correct situation. So every day, everywhere, when you keep your correct situation moment to moment, all the situations in your everyday life are clear. Then any kong-an you test your mind with is your situation just now, and it too will be very clear.

You said that you are studying electronics. This is Zen. Electrical energy can change into anything. Sometimes it makes things hot, sometimes cold; sometimes it makes wind, sometimes light; sometimes it gives the correct time; sometimes it makes food. This original energy has no name and no form. So this energy is like your mind. If you understand one form of electricity then you can understand electricity's substance. When you see a light, do you know where the light comes from? Light is electrical energy; electrical energy is light. Electrical energy is part of our everyday lives. In the same way, your moment-to-moment correct action *is* your true self, clear mind, and the truth. So if you learn the correct way from electricity, no kong-an will stop you.

Your homework answer was "beard." This kong-an is an attack kong-an. How can you defend yourself? You must attack!

In an interview, a Zen Master asks a student, "What color is the wall?"

"White."

Then he asks, "Is that correct?" If you hesitate, just then, you are already dead. It's like fighting. You must attack! When he asks, "Is this correct?" you answer, "Are you hungry?"

If you ask a child, "What is one plus two?" he says, "Three."

"Is that correct?"

"Yes, it's correct." He believes in himself, so he doesn't check himself.

"One plus two doesn't equal three . . ."

"It does too! My teacher said so!" A child's mind doesn't move: no holding onto words or thinking.

If you throw a ball hard against a wall, it comes back hard. Throw it slowly; it comes back slowly. If the Master grabs a sword, you must grab one too! This is reflected action. "What color is the wall?" he asks you. This is a terrible question!

"You already understand."

"I don't."

"No? Then I'll teach you: white!" You must believe in yourself 100%!

When you want to do something and then you don't do it, you don't believe in yourself: you have the head of a dragon but the tail of a snake. So I hope you only go straight—don't know, believe 100% in your everyday life, get Enlightenment, and save all beings from suffering.

Yours in the Dharma,
S. S.

ZEN AND CHRISTIANITY

New York, New York
May 4, 1977

Dear Soen Sa Nim,

We both wanted to tell you again what a joy it was meeting you and being able to work with you for those three days of Yong Maeng Jong Jin in New Haven. I'm deeply grateful to you for that chance, brief though it was, and I hope it will be the first of many.

I told you that there was a little book I wanted to give you, and here it is. This is a small work on contemplative prayer, from five or six hundred years ago, when practice was a living thing in pre-Protestant England. I thought that the title, *The Cloud of Unknowing*, and what the title refers to, might be of some interest to you, and some passages in the book I have, for years, found very beautiful and instructive.

These weeks have been full of travel, to New York and through New England for poetry readings and the meetings with students that go with them. We practiced as and when we could, and I held your words up and tried to become one with them, to the point where they and I would disappear together. Don't know. That's where the homework is at the moment, and I don't say that with apology. That's the answer to the man dropping ashes on the Buddha ("Mind Meal," Sixth Gate) question, right now. I've thought I had answers to it from time to time—but I was *thinking*. Not attached to the answers, but still attached to the thinking. So I don't know.

Please take good care of yourself, for the sake of all beings, and have a good summer.

Hapchang,
William

June 5, 1977

Dear William,

How are you and Dana? Thank you for your letter and also for the book. I am sorry that I am so late in answering; your letter was forwarded from Providence only a short time ago, and then I have been very busy with a big Buddha's Birthday ceremony and Yong Maeng Jong Jins in Los Angeles and Berkeley.

Buddha said that someone who brushes against you in the street does this as a result of sharing karma with you for five hundred lifetimes. So our three days of practicing, eating, and living together mean that we have met and continued to meet for many, many lifetimes—strong karma together. And this will not stop in the future. We will meet again and again, into infinite time. But you and I and all our Dharma friends must remember: what is our direction? This is very important. You and I and our friends sharing the same karma means that our direction is attaining Enlightenment, finishing the great work of life and death, and saving all beings from suffering. This is our great vow. Just as space is infinite, so all beings are infinite. So our great vow is infinite. So together we have entered the ocean of the great Bodhisattva way.

You talked about *The Cloud of Unknowing*. Yes, some Christian mystics have spoken in a way similar to the style of Zen teaching. But most Christian mystics cannot break the wall between God and man. Some say, "Throw away God and all things." This style of speech resembles Zen, but one more step is necessary. If you have God to throw away, you still have God.

I have a student who is an Episcopal priest in Washington, D.C. He sometimes comes to the Providence Zen Center to sit with us. On his invitation I have sometimes taught at the Washington Cathedral, where ministers and Catholic priests have come for Zen practice and interviews. Some talk about God and their true self becoming one; some talk about throwing away God. This means they still have God. I tell them, "If you cannot kill your God, you don't understand true God. True God has no name or form, no speech or words. Many people make God in their minds, so they cannot understand true God. You must kill your God; then you will understand true God. Then Zen and Christianity are the same." So I tell them to take one more step.

Here is a just-like-this kong-an by the great Zen Master Ko Bong, who lived in China seven hundred years ago. He made three gates to test his students' minds.

Ko Bong's Three Gates ("Mind Meal," Seventh Gate)

The first gate: "The sun in the sky shines everywhere. Why does a cloud obscure it?" If you understand this kong-an, you understand Buddha, God, truth, life, karma—everything.

The second gate: "Everyone has a shadow following them. How can you not step on your shadow?" If you understand this kong-an, there will be no problem with any of your actions.

The third gate: "The whole universe is on fire. Through what kind of samadhi can you escape being burned?"

This is a famous kong-an. If you have time, please try it. I hope that you will send me a good answer. If you finish the kong-an, you can go anywhere and stay anywhere.

You are a very busy man, with your travels and readings. But don't lose your head. If you want to find your head, you are a fool. You wrote that you try to become one with my words. This is already a mistake. Put it all down!

And about your homework: you said only don't know. This don't-know is better than a Zen Master, better than God or Buddha. Don't check your mind, don't check your feelings; don't check anything. I hope you only go straight—don't know, soon finish your homework, get Enlightenment, and save all beings from suffering.

Yours in the Dharma,
S. S.

THE FACE IN THE MIRROR

Findhorn, Scotland
November 28, 1976

Dear Soen Sa Nim,

Thank you very much for your letter. It came like the sun at dawn.

Tonight I saw the Buddha in the lid of an ice cream tub.

Between my first sentence and the second I looked up. The face in the mirror looked just like me. What's that?

Best wishes for Christmas and the New Year to you and everyone at P.Z.C.

Love,
Jane

December 15, 1977

Dear Jane,

Thank you for your wonderful letter.

You say you looked in the mirror and said, "Who's that?" In the middle there was the reflection of your face, and also there was your real face. I ask you: the mirror face and your face— which one is the correct face? Are they the same or different?

If you said, "Same," I would hit your face. You would say, "Ouch!" but the mirror face does not feel anything. If you said, "Different," I would tell you that, before you were born, your face was empty; after you die, your face will be empty; so your face is empty. The reflected face is also empty, so the mirror face and your face are the same.

So I ask you one more time, are they the same or different? If you say "Same," you do not understand your original face. Also, if you say "Different," you do not understand your original face. What is your original face?

Long ago, an eminent teacher said, "Don't think good and bad. At that time, what is your original face?" This is a famous kong-an. Don't make anything; then you will get your original face and get everything. If you don't understand your face, only go straight—don't know.

Yours in the Dharma,
S. S.

VII. PRACTICING ZEN
WITH OTHER PEOPLE

PRACTICING ALONE

New York, New York
June 26, 1978

Dear Seung Sahn Soen Sa Nim,

Thank you for your letter and for the picture of Kwan Seum Bosal. Thank you so much for your care.

Please let me take your time to explain something. When I was practicing at another Zen Center I became crazy and caused a lot of confusion and trouble. I went to Yong Maeng Jong Jin held at Bob's house on Long Island last weekend, and again, I found practicing with other people very difficult. It is as if I struggle with some deep barrier; I become very strange with people, so that I cannot really act appropriately and want a lot of special attention. I know that this is not good for other people. I cannot bear to do it, but I can't seem to control it either.

You say that practicing with others will help my bad karma. But I feel as if I would take much more than I could give—that I would be a burden. I do not want to do that again. That is why I have been living and practicing alone. It is so important for me to keep my balance.

George, the Master Dharma Teacher, said none of us is special, especially good or especially bad, but I feel so very different from other people. It is strange. I myself do not understand, and I am sorry. I feel that I must continue my practice alone.

Thank you so much for your concern.

Yours sincerely,
Gail

Dear Gail,

Thank you for your letter. How are you?

I read your letter. I know this kind of thinking. You are not the only person with this kind of karma; many students like practicing alone. This is not good, not bad—better than nothing. But if you practice alone your practice does not grow. When you practice alone, you can lose perspective on your opinions, your condition, and your situation; your ideas only get stronger. You may not understand this growth yourself. If you practice with other people, you will see your karma. Only if you see your karma can you make it disappear.

Zen means not holding onto anything. If you are holding something, or making something, or attached to something, you are not practicing Zen. If you try to practice Zen in this way you cannot get Enlightenment and cannot understand your true self, even if you try for your whole life. So it is very important to put down your ideas and your feelings. What are you? If you don't know, only go straight—don't know.

You are always checking, checking, checking—"my feelings," "somebody's feelings," "my mind," "somebody's understanding." So you make your problems. You say you cannot help other people, and that you are a burden to them. Don't worry about other people. If you practice with others, your good and bad actions already help other people. We call this together action.

Together action is like washing potatoes. When people wash potatoes in Korea, instead of washing them one at a time, they put them all in a tub full of water. Then someone puts a stick in the tub and pushes it up and down, up and down. This makes the potatoes rub against each other; as they bump into each other, the hard crusty dirt falls off. If you wash potatoes one at a time, it takes a long time to clean each one, and only one potato gets clean at a time. If they are all together, the potatoes clean each other.

Our practice of bowing, chanting, and sitting together, and everyone living together is like having many potatoes bumping into each other, cleaning each other. Sometimes in the morning you are tired, so you do not want to get out of bed, or after work you only want to watch television. But when you live at a Zen Center you must practice with everyone; you must put down your own feelings and do together action. This action means not being controlled by your bad karma of desire, anger, or ignorance.

Sometimes you bump into other people: "I don't want to bow!" or "I'm too tired to do the dishes!" But soon you see you are only bumping into your bad karma. If you are alone, it's easy to hold your own ideas. When you are separate from other people, your thinking and opinions grow stronger and stronger. Then your mind becomes narrow and tight; it has many walls.

Zen means inside and outside become one. This means at any time, you and your correct situation become one. When you practice with other people, everyone helps you see your correct situation. Then your life becomes simple and clear. Then your thinking-walls become weaker and weaker, and soon they disappear. Then you can see and you can hear; everything is the truth, just as it is. Then when someone is happy, you are happy with them. When someone is sad, you perceive their sadness and help them. That is called freedom. It is also called great love, great compassion, and the great Bodhisattva way.

If you practice alone, you only make your own walls. When will you get out of your small walls? This universe is very wide, infinite in time and space. So don't make "my space"; don't make "my time." Put down I-my-me. Only try, try, try. This is very important. The first time is very difficult, but if you don't check your mind, don't check your feelings, don't check your understanding, then no problem. Thinking comes and goes—let it be.

When you practice correctly and become strong, your

demons can also become strong. When together action is difficult, this means your Dharma and your karma are both very strong. At that time, you must only go straight—don't know and persevere. Then you will win, O.K.? Then no problem. But if your demons become stronger than your Dharma, then your persevering mind can become weak, and you become crazy. So you must try, try, try. If you keep try-mind, you will become a great woman.

So I hope you only go straight—don't know, don't hold your feelings, get Enlightenment, and save all beings from suffering.

Yours in the Dharma,
S. S.

PRACTICING TOGETHER

Berkeley, California
November 22, 1977

Dear Soen Sa Nim,

Thank you very much for introducing me to Diana and Ezra. I like them and everyone else here at the Berkeley Zen Center very much.

Something funny has happened. Yesterday morning I was reading through the kong-an book and I wondered why so many people wrote you letters. After all, you always say, "Only go straight—don't know," so why are letters necessary? Then, last night, a situation came up, and I suddenly felt the need to write to you. Instant karma!

As you know, Michael is living here at the Zen Center. When he first moved in, he was practicing hard and gave a lot of energy to the Center. About two weeks ago, though, he got a job in San Francisco and has been drifting away from us ever since, missing most of our morning and evening practice.

Yesterday was the worst. He was supposed to cook dinner but forty-five minutes before dinner, nobody had seen or heard from him, so we went ahead and made dinner ourselves. He came home five minutes before evening meditation practice, completely unconcerned that he was late. Practice had a funny feeling to it. After practice, we all sat down and talked.

One thing Michael said, which he's been saying for the last two weeks, is that he didn't see why it made any difference whether or not he was here, as long as he was practicing just-now mind wherever he was. We tried to explain to him that when you live in a Zen Center, it is very important to do together action, and that his doing his bows in San Francisco and our doing them here wasn't together action.

All my life I have wanted to be a teacher and have taught people whenever I could, but until I met you, I had nothing of importance to teach. Yesterday I was faced with a situation in which I needed to teach someone, but I could not see clearly enough to do it. Last night, Michael talked about leaving. I could see that no matter what happened, this situation was teaching the Zen Center and teaching me; it showed me that I have to practice harder.

For the last two weeks, we have all been checking Michael, forming opinions about him. Then when we all talked to him, I think everyone managed to put down their opinions, only wanting to help. Today, Michael decided to stay at the Zen Center; he has "fixed" himself; we didn't have to do anything, only put our opinions down. Before, I had an intellectual understanding of how opinions could get in the way of clear mind. Now, I see that not only do opinions create a hindrance for me, but that my opinions can be a hindrance to someone else! It has now become very important for me to do hard training and put down opinions, likes and dislikes, checking. I reread the Temple Rules [Appendix II] this morning, and suddenly, they make a lot more sense than they have in the past. How can I thank you and Michael enough for this teaching?

Homework: A man drops ashes on the Buddha ("Mind Meal," Sixth Gate). I stand the Buddha on its head and bow to it.

Putting down all opinions,
how can mind be a hindrance?
When red comes, only red.
Yesterday, it was raining;
Today, the clouds break up and the sun shines down.

Gratefully,
Jeff

December 5, 1977

Dear Jeff,

Thank you for your letter. How are you and the Berkeley Zen Center family?

You said I introduced you to Diana and Ezra, but this is your karma with Diana and Ezra from many previous lifetimes. In previous lives you made karma together, so now you live in the same house and do the same practice together; you are happy and lucky; you fight, check, and help other people together. Most important, if you can control your good and bad karma from moment to moment, then you can use it to save all beings. But if you cannot control your karma, then it will control you, not only in this life but for numberless lifetimes in the future, making good and bad, happiness and sadness, and leading you around and around. This is called the wheel of suffering.

You talked about Michael. This is very interesting—a good example of correct practicing. There are three kinds of people. At the lowest level are the people who cannot control themselves. For these people, together action, living together, and practicing together is very important. They must only follow the sangha. Sometimes, if their likes and dislikes are strong, their karma will appear, but if they continue to practice and do together action, their strong like-and-dislike karma will weaken, and finally there will be no hindrance to together action. Keeping a clear mind, moment to moment, will be very easy.

For someone at this first level, the whole sangha is his teacher. Michael is sometimes this kind of student. He is a very good person, likes together action, and understands what the correct way is. But occasionally his bad karma appears and since his head is very clever and his cleverness sometimes controls him, then he doesn't like together action. At those times he says, "Practicing is not important. Everything is O.K., so it doesn't matter what I do." This mind is very dangerous. A very clever person can have this kind of opinion. This kind of person has many problems inside, but outside he can justify anything he does. So it is very important for this person to do together action, so he can clean his karma. Then it is possible for his inside ideas and his outside actions to become one.

At the next level, there are people for whom together action is no problem. But, if these people go outside alone and hear or see something, their minds still move. If they are by themselves in a quiet place or in the mountains, practicing alone is no problem. In a bad situation, however, they cannot control their situation. With hard training, they can get Dharma energy and they will become high-class students.

High-class students' minds do not move in any situation, alone or with other people. In a bad situation, they do bad action together with others, but they only act together on the outside. Inside, they have great love and compassion. So, any place, any time, any situation, any condition is no hindrance. When the time is right they can teach the correct way.

You said you want to teach other people. So you must become a high-class student. I think on the inside you already are a high-class student — no problem — so you can teach Michael. You said that Michael changed his mind and will continue to stay at Berkeley Zen Center. His going or staying, having a problem or not, acting together or not, and finally his good and bad action are all your true teachers.

You said that if you keep your opinion, you cannot help other people. That is correct. If you follow the situation moment to moment, then you will find your correct opinion and condition. This is the source of wisdom and Bodhisattva action. If you have this mind, the Temple Rules are not necessary for you. The Temple Rules are very important for first-level students; middle-class and high-class students *use* the Temple Rules to teach other people.

Your answer to the cigarette-man kong-an is, "I stand the Buddha on its head and bow to it." Then this man says, "Oh wonderful, wonderful! How are you, Dharma friend?" Then what? You cannot fix his mind. He likes your action; this means you and he are the same. But how do you *fix* his mind? How do you teach him like-this and just-like-this? This is most important. Give me a good answer. Hurry up! Hurry up! Time will not wait for you.

Your poem is very, very wonderful. Here is a poem for you:

> Opinions are the truth when you don't hold them.
> Hindrance and no hindrance are not my job.
> How many colors are there in the rainbow?
> The dog likes the bone.
> Children like candy.
> What do you like?

> Yours in the Dharma,
> S. S.

YOUR GASOLINE IS INEXHAUSTIBLE

Ann Arbor, Michigan
November 28, 1977

Dear Soen Sa Nim,

I am a student of Aitken Roshi's who was at the Yong Maeng Jong Jin at the New York Zen Center, November 25-27. Aitken Roshi recommended that I go to your Zen Center. Thank you very much. I am grateful for the chance to meet with you.

Where do you come from?
I clap with both hands.

There are a million sanghas.
The sangha in Hawaii,
The sangha in New York . . .

There is only one sangha
There is no sangha.

When I heard you chant,
I then knew where all Korean music came from.

Chanting in the morning, chanting in
the evening,
The Kayageum sanjo plays for
one moment.

I awake to the silent bell
in the morning.

Soen Sa Nim, I am going to school here in Michigan. How can I keep practicing Zen? It is difficult because there is no group to practice with. I try to sit alone, but my gasoline still runs out. I hope to see you again.

Aloha,
Peggy

Dear Peggy,

Thank you for your letter. How are you?

It was nice to meet you at the Chogye International Zen Center of New York. It is wonderful to have Aitken Roshi's students visiting our Zen Centers and practicing with us. Aitken Roshi is a great Zen Master.

Your poem is very, very wonderful. Here is a poem for you:

Coming and going empty-handed.
The clapping sound comes from where?
No ear, no sound, then what?
Careful! Careful! Don't touch the fishing hook.

The thought, "a million sanghas is no sangha—"
Immediately, the sleep-demon pushes head down.
Sound of waves in Hawaii pulls all the Sangha's minds.
Noise of traffic in New York tears all the sangha's minds.
Be clear! Be clear!

Long ago, a great man saw a fish swimming in the water,
Made "Oe San" (fish mountain) melody.
Kayageum sanjo, yoeng san gok, ta ryeong*
All comes from that.
Dung, dung, daeng, daeng, la, la, la, la.

I'm glad to hear that you're going to school. You said that practicing Zen alone is very difficult. But practicing Zen means, what is your just-now situation? You have no together action. This is a difficult situation. But a bad situation is a good situation; a good situation is a bad situation. You must understand this.

You said your gasoline runs out, but your gasoline is inexhaustible. When you bow, when you sit, your inexhaustible gasoline supply appears. No problem. You must *do* it. You can do everything. If you make difficult, you have difficult. If you

---

* The finest Buddhist music played on the Kayageum sanjo.

make no gasoline, you have no gasoline. If you make gasoline, you have gasoline. Never stop your car; this is most important. Stopping your car means checking your mind and your feelings and everything. So perceive your situation, then only go straight—don't know. Then your gasoline is like a geyser—no problem.

I hope you only go straight—don't know, which is clear like space, never stop your car, finish the great work of life and death, and save all beings from suffering.

Yours in the Dharma,
S. S.

DREAM OF A FORSAKEN JOURNEY

Boston, Massachusetts
April 31, 1977

Dear Soen Sa Nim,

I had a dream last night. A few friends and I set out on a journey. We arrived at the home of a powerful witch who granted all our desires. I received the perfect woman. Quite content, we remained a long time, until we awoke to realize that we had forsaken our journey. The witch refused our request to leave, so we decided to escape. But wherever we went, the witch always managed to remain on our trail. We soon realized that if we wished to leave, we had to return everything she had given us—nothing belonged to us, even my perfect woman. Once everything was returned, she disappeared, and we were free to travel on.

Munindra came to visit at the house in which I live. Ram Das frequents the house regularly. This is a very interesting place to observe the diversity of Dharma paths. I have had a taste of some, but I'll hold onto the straightforward path of "What am I?" This is the right place for me, though. I have learned much here, and there is much more to learn. I have no regrets about moving out of the Zen Center, but I hope to give some lectures at the Zen Center soon.

I hope you are well.

Fred

September 21, 1977

Dear Fred,

How are you? Thank you for your letter and beautiful card.

In your letter, you talk about a dream. That is a wonderful dream. But a dream is a dream. If you hold this dream, you are a dream man. Here is a poem for you:

Guest talking about his dream.
Host also talking about his dream.
Guest, host, together talking about dreams.
They don't understand they are in a dream.
That is a dream.

So, I tell you, you must wake up from your dream!

Many styles of Dharma come and go at your house. That is wonderful. But if you don't understand your True Way, then even Buddha or God coming to your house become your demons. You say, "I have learned much." Remember that understanding and feeling cannot help you. You say you have had a taste of some Dharma paths; also, you say "What am I?" is the way. But if you hold onto any taste, any ideas, then your "What am I?" cannot become strong.

Both thinking and dream are the actions of your consciousness. Dreaming is very simple—it is the action of your seventh and eighth consciousnesses. The seventh and eighth consciousnesses are not limited by time and space. So in your dreams, it is very easy to visit New York, Korea, or Los

Angeles. But in daytime dreams, we have our sixth consciousness, which is our connection to our eyes, our ears, our nose, our tongue, and our body. So in our daytime existence we are limited by time and space.

Nighttime dreaming is very interesting: Zoom, go! Zoom, come! But in daytime dreams, changing your situation is not so easy. Sometimes there is crying and great suffering. In daytime dreams there are many hindrances. So you must wake up. To wake up you must only go straight—don't know.

"Only go straight—don't know" means no form, no feelings, no perceptions, no impulses, no consciousness. Also, no eyes, no ears, no nose, no tongue, no body, no mind, which means no color, no sound, no smell, no taste, no touch, no object of mind. If you have no object of mind, already you are complete; you become absolute. Then boom! You wake up. Then you can see, you can hear, you can smell; everything, just like this, is truth. This truth is not dependent on any Dharma Teacher. Zen means believing in yourself 100%.

To attain absolute mind, you must control your karma. I understand your karma—you like many tastes. For you to learn to control your karma, living at a Zen Center is very necessary. Living at a Zen Center means practicing with other people, putting down I-my-me moment to moment to moment. Then everything is your teacher.

I think from reading your letter that your mind still has likes and dislikes. What do you want?

If you want the True Way, you must put down all likes and dislikes in your mind. If you don't want your true self, then that is O.K. Only, I ask you, what are you doing now? If you are doing something, you must *do* it. Don't make dreams.

I hope you only go straight—don't know, control your karma, keep a mind which is clear like space, soon get Enlightenment, and save all beings from suffering.

Yours in the Dharma,
S. S.

MAKING THE GREAT DHARMA OCEAN

Lawrence, Kansas
March 2, 1978

Dear Soen Sa Nim,

Thank you for your last letter. You, the Berkeley people, and the Cambridge people are in my thoughts.

Wonderful news! There is a strong Zen practice here! It started about a month ago, and I found out about it two weeks ago. There are two students of Maezumi Roshi, one student of Eido Roshi, one student of Philip Kapleau, me, and several people who have never met a Zen Master but are strong sitters. We have not found all of our practice forms yet but it is being worked out with good humor, and everyone is very happy to sit with so many people. There were about a dozen of us last night. So far, we've been meeting two nights a week, but starting tonight, we will try making it five nights.

As you know, when I came out here, I never dreamed I would find any sangha, much less a strong one. After practice, people are so happy to be sitting with each other that nobody wants to leave. Soon we will become used to it and then it will be like brushing teeth, and that will truly be wonderful.

Much love,
Judy

March 14, 1978

Dear Judy,

Thank you for your letter. How are you and all your Dharma friends?

In your letter, you said you are practicing together with students from many centers. That is wonderful. If you each make

I-my-me disappear, then you will learn from each other and teach each other. Sometimes having people from different Zen schools is better than everyone being from one school. If people only keep their tradition and their style very strongly and don't like together action, then they have a little problem. But if there are people in your group like this, these people teach everyone in the group and also learn from the group. It is very important that "my idea," "my condition," and "my situation" disappear. Then your correct opinion, correct condition, and correct situation appear. If you keep this mind, then in any place, with any students, and with any style, together action is no problem. That is Zen, and great Bodhisattva action. You already understand this.

Many kinds of rivers flow into the ocean. Once in the ocean, all the separate river waters disappear and only become ocean water. Each river cannot keep its own situation and condition. An eminent teacher said, "The Great Way is like the ocean." I hope you make the Great Dharma Ocean, that everyone flows into your Dharma Ocean, and gets enough-mind, which is great love, great compassion, and the great Bodhisattva way.

Yours in the Dharma,
S. S.

VIII. TEACHER AND STUDENT

SHOPPING FOR A TEACHER

January 10, 1977

Dear Soen Sa Nim,

How are you? I hope you are well.

I was sitting at the Insight Meditation Center in Barre, Mass. when you came to visit. Your talk helped me with my practice there.

I have some questions to which I hope you can find the time to respond.

What do you think of the Vipassana as taught at the Insight Meditation Center? Is it good to stay with one form of practice or to go to many teachers and many teachings?

I like the Zen you teach because it makes me keep don't-know mind. But I find the Zen form confusing. Do I have to understand Zen talk and Zen form to learn from your teaching?

It is asked, "If all things return to the One, where does the One return?" But, I would like to ask you—why did all things leave the One in the first place?

I think that I have asked enough questions. I look forward to seeing you at the March Yong Maeng Jong Jin in Providence. Thank you.

Pax,
Steven

January 19, 1977

Dear Steven,

How are you? Thank you for your letter. You say that my talk has helped you. That is wonderful. I am happy to hear you will be coming to Yong Maeng Jong Jin.

You asked me if Vipassana meditation is good or bad. If you are thinking, then it is very bad. If you have cut off all thinking, then it is not bad. Good and bad are in your mind, not in Vipassana meditation. What do you want? That is very important.

To answer your next question: when people go to the market, some of them want soap, others want clothes, others want food. They are there only for what they want; other things are not necessary for these people.

Each teacher has a direction and a teaching style. If you find a teacher with the same direction as yours, then follow that teacher. If you have no direction, then you will only go around and around from teacher to teacher. So again, what do you want? This is very important.

If you want to practice Zen, then you must learn Zen practice style. If you don't want to practice Zen, then Zen style is not necessary. Very simple. What is important is the reason *why* you practice. Once you understand why you practice, finding a teacher will be no problem. Then a teacher's style will not hinder you. Maybe you won't understand everything about the style, but you will understand your teacher's direction, so you will just try.

You ask why all beings left the One. I answer you that if you make one, I will hit you thirty times, and if you make 10,000, I will also hit you thirty times. Don't make one. Don't make anything. Then you will get everything. I hope you only go straight—don't know, find your direction, get Enlightenment, and save all beings from suffering.

See you soon,
S. S.

WILD DHARMA SCENES
AND BROKEN PRECEPTS

Boulder, Colorado
July 26, 1977

Dear Soen Sa Nim,

I hope you are well. Please, as much as possible, try to take care of your body.

I have not seen you in a while. I, too, have been traveling around teaching the Dharma. How is the family on the East Coast?

I am still living with Paulette. She is well and continuing to study with her teacher. Her teacher is very good, very crazy. Many of his students think they have complete freedom to do what they want. There are many drunken parties, and the observation of precepts is practically nil. For me, it is good teaching to see such wild Dharma scenes: it surely helps cut my ideas about good and bad Dharma. Nonetheless, I am generally pretty sober—drunken freedom doesn't appeal to me.

Nowadays, I am feeling strong in body and mind. It is easy to forget myself. I am joyed by the Bodhisattva Way.

May all beings be happy and liberated.

Much love to you and our Dharma family,

Richard

August 4, 1977

Dear Richard,

Thank you for your letter. How are you and Paulette? You worry about my body, but it is strong—no problem.

Paulette's studying with her teacher is not good, not bad—

this type of Buddhism is wonderful practicing. But the precepts are very important.

When Buddha was dying, Mahakasyapa and another great disciple asked him, "When you die, we will have no teacher. How can we continue practicing? How can we control the sangha?"

Buddha said, "I have already given you the precepts. The precepts are your teacher. If you practice correctly and keep the precents correctly, you can control the sangha and help them find the true way."

So, the precepts are very important. If you keep the precepts, they will be your teacher, but if you break the precepts, you kill your teacher. If you get Enlightenment, your direction is unmoving, so keeping or not keeping the precepts doesn't matter: you will always do Bodhisattva action. But if you still have karma, if you cannot control your karma, then freedom action will arise from ignorance and only make more bad karma. When will you get out of the ocean of life and death?

The Avatamsaka Sutra says, "Drinking and sex are no-hindrance Prajna." In other words, when you can control your karma—your desire, anger, and ignorance—then any action is no problem: whatever action you do will teach other people. My teacher, Zen Master Ko Bong, taught this way.

At Jung Hae Sa Temple in Korea, the schedule consists of three months of sitting followed by three months of vacation. During vacation, everyone collects money or food and brings it back for the sitting period. When Zen Master Mang Gong, my grand-teacher, was just beginning the temple, there was no money at all. The students would go around to the homes of lay people, recite the heart sutra, get rice or money, and return to the monastery. But when my teacher Ko Bong got rice, he'd sell it at the end of the day and go out drinking. Everyone else came back at the end of a vacation with sacks of rice. All Ko Bong brought back was wine. When he was full of wine, he was also full of complaints, "This temple is no good! Mang Gong doesn't understand anything! He's low-class!"

Once Zen Master Mang Gong showed up during one of Ko Bong's tirades and screamed at him, "What do you understand?" Everybody was waiting to see what would happen. "KO BONG!!!"

"Yes?"

"Why are you always insulting me behind my back?"

Ko Bong looked completely surprised and offended. "Zen Master! I never said anything about you! I was talking about this good-for-nothing Mang Gong!"

"Mang Gong? What do you mean, Mang Gong? I'M MANG GONG! What's the difference between Mang Gong and me?"

"KAAAATZ!" Ko Bong yelled, loud enough to split everyone's ear drums. That ended it.

"Go sleep it off," Mang Gong said, and he left the room.

My teacher was always drunk, used abusive speech, and showed disrespectful behavior. But he always kept a clear mind. "Mang Gong? What's the difference between Mang Gong and me? "KAAATZ!" That katz is very important—better than money or bags of rice. Ko Bong completely believed in himself.

If you believe completely in yourself, your actions will teach other people. Also you will be able to do any action to help other people. This is the great Bodhisattva way.

There are four kinds of Bodhisattva action. First, there is giving things to people who don't have something they want or need. Next, there is speaking kindly to people and showing love for them. Then there is talking about the Dharma. But if people don't listen, then you must act together with them. Together action means if they like sex, have sex together; if they like drinking, drink together; if they like songs, sing together with them. Without any desire for yourself, your actions are only for other people. Finally, when suffering comes, they will listen to you and you can teach them.

If you have great love, then in any situation you will not be hindered by desire, anger, and ignorance. But if you do not yet have this Bodhisattva mind, then you must first attain your true self. This is very necessary.

If we are controlled by desire, anger, and ignorance, we cannot find our true way. If we keep our correct situation, moment to moment, our just-now mind becomes stronger. When we are confused or cannot control ourselves, the Precepts show us what our correct situation is. So I will give you homework:

Nam Cheon Kills a Cat ("Mind Meal," Ninth Gate)

Once the monks of the eastern and western halls of the monastery were disputing about a cat. Master Nam Cheon, holding up the cat and pulling out his precepts knife, said, "You! Give me one word and I will save this cat! If you cannot, I will kill it!" No one could answer. Finally, Nam Cheon killed the cat. In the evening, when Jo Ju returned to the temple, Nam Cheon told him of the incident. Jo Ju took off his shoe, put it on his head, and walked away. Nam Cheon said, "If you had been there, I could have saved the cat."

Nam Cheon said, "Give me one word!" At that time, what can you do?

Jo Ju put his shoe on his head. What does this mean?

If you attain Nam Cheon's Bodhisattva Mind, then you understand keeping and breaking the Precepts.

I hope you always keep a mind which is clear like space, believe completely in yourself, get Enlightenment, and save all beings from suffering.

Yours in the Dharma,
S. S.

BETTER THAN A ZEN MASTER

Chicago, Illinois
September 12, 1977

Dear Soen Sa Nim,

It is nice to hear that you'll be visiting in October. It will be good to see you. But, there doesn't seem to be any great enthusiasm for semiannual talks from a Master. We are looking for a meditation master who can reside here full-time, and around whom a deeper or more extensive practice can form. We have reached the point where we can offer a place to live and teach, and a living stipend, when we are lucky enough to find such a person.

If you can help us locate such a person, we would be very grateful.

A long Yong Maeng Jong Jin would attract a good number of people, I would say.

I hope you are well.

Best regards,
Richard

October 7, 1977

Dear Richard,

How are you? Thank you for your letter.

This answer is late: I am sorry. I have been teaching at Tahl Mah Sah in Los Angeles, and in Berkeley. My students, Diana and Ezra Clark, have just made their home in Berkeley into a Zen Center, so I visit them and do Yong Maeng Jong Jin with them.

I wanted to visit Chicago, but at this time it is not possible. I am sorry. I cannot help Chicago students now, but maybe I can help you in the future. Some of my students in other cities have already started Zen Centers. Now these Zen Centers need my help so they can become strong. Then I could help a Chicago Zen Center. But you said you want a full-time Zen Master. That is a wonderful idea. If you find a great Zen Master, you must try.

I know your mind. Your mind did not get enough of my teaching. Do you know the story of Na Mak Ho Hyan Zen Master? He was the Seventh Patriarch in China. When he first visited the Sixth Patriarch, Hui Neng, he said, "Please teach me the Dharma. I am Ho Hyan from Seung Sahn Mountain."

Hui Neng said, "What thing is here from Seung Sahn Mountain?"

Ho Hyan did not understand at all, so he kept this don't-know mind, left Hui Neng's temple, and returned to Seung Sahn Mountain where he only sat for eight years. Finally, he got Enlightenment. He went back to Hui Neng, bowed to him, and said, "If you say one thing it is not a bull's-eye." When Hui Neng heard this, he understood that Ho Hyan had attained Enlightenment. Soon, Ho Hyan received transmission and became the Seventh Patriarch.

Long ago many great Zen students visited a Zen Master only once, returned to their homes, practiced and then they attained great Enlightenment. If you have a correct only-go-straight, don't-know mind, then any Zen Master, any sutra, any Bodhisattva is already yours. However, your mind wants something, so you want a Zen Master.

I think you are a very good student. But you want something, so you have a problem. Put down this "want-mind." So I ask you, what are you? If you don't know, only go straight—don't know. This don't-know mind is better than a Zen Master, better than Buddha, better than God, better than anything.

I hope you only go straight—don't know, keep a mind which is clear like space, get Enlightenment, and save all beings from suffering.

Yours in the Dharma,
S. S.

YOUR IDEAS ARE YOUR CAGE

August 3, 1977

Dear Soen Sa Nim,

After much consideration, sadness, and pain I have decided to resign as a Dharma Teacher. I would very much like to maintain my personal relationship with you, but only as an individual, not as a Dharma Teacher. During the Dharma Teacher weekend, it became much clearer what a good Dharma Teacher is. I do not seem to satisfy most of the requirements—so being a Dharma Teacher is a huge burden for me. Right from the start, my karma has been far away from ceremony, organizations, Dharma combat, kong-ans. With time, this distance only grows. I was very happy to see so much joy and energy among all the Dharma Teachers during the weekend. However, it only served to give me a stronger sense of my distance from it all.

My decision to leave would have been a lot easier if it were not for the immense love and respect for you as a person and teacher, and for the purity and power of your ultimate, primary teaching. You are the finest teacher I have ever had, but nevertheless, I feel that I must walk alone. "Believe in yourself" may mean for me facing the fear that comes from throwing away "I am a professor" and now, "I am a Zen Dharma Teacher."

Please do not worry about me—I feel very strong, but also sad at having to let go. I will be going on a hundred-day retreat soon. I will see you in person before that to talk it over and return my robes.

Thank you for your ever-present love and generosity.

Yours in the Dharma,
Andrew

August 12, 1977

Dear Andrew,

How are you? Thank you for your beautiful letter. Your mind is very sad; my mind is also very sad.

Your mind has many hindrances. Also I am a hindrance to you. You will stop being a Dharma Teacher and return your robe and bowls. This is an outside action. But I always ask you, "What is most important? Why do you live in the world? Why are you practicing? Why are you doing a retreat? What do you teach? What are you?" If you have an answer, tell me. If you cannot answer, you must make I-my-me disappear.

You said that you understand your karma. But you don't understand your karma. If you correctly understand your karma, it is possible to make your karma disappear. You only hold onto your karma and make it your treasure. This is ignorance and illusion.

I like you very much, but you don't listen to me. Don't *make* anything! If you make complications, you have complications. If you don't make anything, your mind is empty. Then nothing will be a hindrance. Your saying that your Karma is far from something means that you make something in your mind and are strongly holding onto it. You cannot fix this mind if you do a hundred-day retreat, or a thousand-day retreat, or a whole-life retreat—you will not find your true way.

Returning your Dharma Teacher robe and bowls to me is just more holding onto your ideas. I always say to you that you must make "my opnion," "my condition," "my situation" disappear. Then, your correct opinion, correct condition, and correct situation will appear.

You once gave a beautiful Dharma speech about a bear in a cage. It is a wonderful story.

Once there was a great black bear who lived in the mountains. He was happy and free; when he wasn't sleeping, he spent much of his time searching for food. Sometimes he found some, and sometimes he didn't. That was his life.

One day some men came and captured him, and they took him to a large circus where they locked him in a small cage. Soon an animal trainer taught him to perform circus tricks. Each time the bear performed a trick correctly, he would be fed. The rest of the time, he just walked back and forth in his cage. It was a small cage, so he got to know it very well. He always had enough food, and soon he forgot about his life in the mountains.

One night after several years had passed, some vandals crept into the circus and broke open all the animal cages. The bear was suddenly free, and he left the circus and found his way back to the mountains that had once been his home. But the mountains were now unfamiliar, and it was not easy for him to find food. So he began turning somersaults forwards and backwards, forwards and backwards. Some other bears watched him for a while and then asked what he was doing. "Oh," he replied, "I'm doing tricks so that I'll get food."

"You rock-head!" they laughed. "You're in the mountains. Who is going to bring you food for turning somersaults? You must find it yourself!"

This bear had become so attached to his cage that he had forgotten all about freedom. Everyone does this. Everyone has a cage that they have become attached to—a doctor's cage, a lawyer's cage, a professor's cage, a job cage, a friendship cage, a family cage. People live in these cages and so they don't really understand freedom. This means they don't understand the rest of the world. They only understand life in their cage.

Now your head is like that bear's head. You like your cage so you say, "I am strong"; this means, "my cage is strong." By saying, "no more Dharma Teacher," you are saying to me, "don't come into my cage." But I want to break your cage and make you completely free and a great man. So, I am very sad that you are making your cage stronger. Someday your cage will not be strong, and then I can help you. If you put down your holding-mind, then your cage will disappear. That holding-mind is "I." You must kill your "I." This is very necessary.

You must understand that $1 - 1 = 0$. Very simple, not difficult. If you don't understand this arithmetic, you must return to elementary school. You understand too much. How much does this understanding help you? You do yoga every day. Why do you do yoga? This *why* is important. Only for your body? Only for your life? Only for your mind? Only for the truth? Which one?

For you and me, our lives will soon be finished. Who is guaranteeing your life? What do you want? You already have everything. But you cannot wake up from your dream. So I say to you: Wake up! Wake up! Only go straight—don't know. Don't make anything. Don't hold onto anything. Don't worry about a robe and bowls. You say to me you want to do a hundred-day retreat. If you want to talk about your retreat before you go, that's fine. Then after your hundred-day retreat, we'll meet again and talk about being a Dharma Teacher. You say, "I am strong; don't worry." I cannot stop: I am very worried about you.

I hope you only go straight—don't know, kill your small self, keep a mind which is clear like space, then soon finish the great work of life and death and get complete freedom, become a great man, and save all beings from suffering.

Yours in the Dharma,
S. S.

A DREAM OF LETTING GO

Dear Soen Sa Nim,

I guess you heard that we received notice to move Tahl Mah Zen Center out of our current building by July 18. Although we have to move in a hurry, we decided to stay together if possible. We tried to find a place all week long. Right now we are unable to find a house, and we must live separately until something comes up. We are all sad that the Zen Center is not together and that we must practice separately.

Now I am living with Pam and we are bowing and sitting in the mornings and at night in our small apartment—but I miss the company of other people.

A few weeks ago I had an interesting dream. I've had similar dreams for a few years, but this time it was different. Usually, I dream that someone is trying to kill or hurt me and I am trying to yell for help, but no sound comes out. I am aware that I am sleeping and know that if I can force myself to wake up, everything will be O.K. I usually do this and wake up with a start, drenched in sweat and feeling very afraid. But this time I dreamt that someone was trying to hurt me, but instead of trying to get help to get out of the situation, the mind that is aware that I'm asleep suddenly told me that there was another way of dealing with the situation. It said to my sleeping self, "Let go—stop fighting—die, if necessary," and I felt myself relax and just let happen what would happen. I woke up a little later, not scared, and not drenched in sweat. Isn't it funny how even when we see aspects of ourselves that we know are selfish and ugly, we still cling to them? Dying to those things is not easy—and yet, what other way is there?

That's all for now. Take good care of yourself, and say hello to all at Providence for me. Hope to see you soon.

Sincerely,
Alicia

Dear Alicia,

How are you and your Dharma friends? Thank you for your interesting letter.

See Hoy just came to the Dharma Teacher Yong Maeng Jong Jin and told me the same thing you did about the Tahl Mah Sah Zen Center situation. A bad situation is a good situation; a good situation is a bad situation. Now, you are all living separately and practicing separately and there are some problems finding a new place. But you have the correct situation, so any problems are good teaching for you.

If you have no direction, any problem is a big problem and brings much suffering, but our practicing is only go straight—don't check I-my-me. Then bad situations, good situations, and big problems are all good teachers. Everything is no problem.

I read your letter. You are very strong. Wonderful. You are a strong and wonderful Zen student. Maybe soon we'll get a new house and can gather together again and practice together again. Now we are having a bad time. But don't make "bad time." Then you will have a good time. So only go straight—don't make anything. Then you will get everything.

In the whole world, everything is changing, changing, but everything, moment to moment, is perfectly complete. That means that your mind is complete, everything is complete, and also that each moment is complete. If your mind is not complete, everything is not complete, so every moment is a big problem. Not complete means making something. Complete means not making anything. Already, everything is perfect. So, I say to you, only go straight—don't know.

You had a dream. Earlier, after your dreams, you sweated a lot and were very afraid. Now, you don't sweat and are not afraid. So I say to you that is wonderful! This means your bad karma has disappeared that much, and you are that much stronger. Dreaming is the action of the seventh and eighth consciousnesses. Before, you made something. This something stays in your eighth consciousness, and at night, your sixth consciousness separates from your seventh and eighth consciousnesses. All bad and good karma is kept in your eighth consciousness. Somebody has a lot of bad karma, so every night, this person has bad dreams. Somebody has a lot of good karma, so every night he has good dreams. But these dreams originally are empty—nothing. If you keep nothing-mind for a long time, good and bad disappear and your consciousness is very clear.

Your dream was bad, but you have control. That means your mind is becoming clear. So only go straight—don't know. Then your mind will become more clear, so controlling your life will also be no problem. Then you will understand dreams. Then you will understand the correct way.

Long ago in China, there were five schools of Zen: Rinzai, Soto, Poep An, Un Mun, and E An. E An and An Sahn together made one school. E An was the teacher, An Sahn the disciple. Once E An was asleep. At that time An Sahn was only his secretary. He happened to open the door, saw that the Zen Master was asleep, and slowly closed the door. The Zen Master woke up and said, "Just now, I had a dream. Do you understand?"

An Sahn said, "Yes, just now I understand," and washed the Zen Master's face with water. The Master said, "Oh, thank you for washing my face." Then another disciple, Haeng Om, who later became a Zen Master, came into the Zen Master's room. The Master said, "We were just talking about my dream. Do you understand my dream?"

Haeng Om said, "Yes, sir," and went into the kitchen, and brought in some tea. The Zen Master said, "Ah, my students are very wonderful. You all understand my dream."

What does it mean? If you wake up, you wash your face. Then you drink tea. This is the correct way. If you completely understand dreams, then you understand the correct way.

You must understand that this whole world is a dream. Then your desire is a dream, your anger is a dream, and your life is also a dream. You must understand dreams; then you will have no desire for yourself and will act only for all people. Then you have a Bodhisattva dream—only help other people. But understanding is not enough; you must attain the dream. Then you will understand your true self.

My body is very strong, no problem. Everyone at the Providence Zen Center says hello to you. I hope you only go straight—don't know, attain the dream, get Enlightenment, and save all beings from suffering.

Yours in the Dharma,
S. S.

PICTURE TEACHING

Washington, D.C.
December 1, 1976

Dear Soen Sa Nim,

I just wanted to tell you how much I enjoyed the workshop presented by you and your Dharma Teachers in Washington. It has been a long time since I have been in such company.

Being unaware of the rituals of practice, I have sent for a tape and robe and plan on doing a little homework before the New York Yong Maeng Jong Jin.

A child in a gloriously strange land;
Sniffing the flowers and
Eating the trees.

Thank you for accepting me as your student.

Merrie

December 15, 1976

Dear Merrie,

Your poem is very interesting, but I don't understand the meaning. The last words, "Eating the trees"—what does this mean? Who is eating the trees? How are the trees being eaten?

Here is a poem for you:

> Two mud cows together sumo wrestling
> Pull each other around, around, around,
> And into the ocean.

> Which is the winner? Which is the loser?
> No news.

> Seagulls are flying over the water.
> The ocean is blue.

> > Yours in the Dharma,
> > S. S.

December 27, 1976

Dear Soen Sa Nim,

First lessons in any new language are always slow and practice is needed to become proficient. So here is my practice so far:

> To learn to swim,
> Get in the water!

> > Beneath the trash heap lies the True Master
> > Do not cart away the trash!
> > Find the True Master,
> > And the trash heap disappears.

> How joyfully disappointing!
> It was always under my nose!
> But I, looking for something else,
> Missed it! . . .

Nothing special!
Nothing different!

At first there are Rules
And . . . Rules
And now . . .

Nothing!!!

But . . .

Rules.

I asked the True Master, "Why am I here?"
"To teach," came the reply.
"To teach what?"
"You already know!"
"But I don't know how!!"
"That's all right, Soen Sa Nim will teach you how."

The fish in the pond,
Merrie

December 30, 1976

Dear Merrie,

Thank you for your letter and the wonderful poem. Your poem is very smooth and beautiful, but you touch only the head and only the foot. Where is your body? Where are your arms?

Long ago, the great Zen Master Ko Bong said to his students every day:

"Here is a poem for you. In the poem, if you find one sentence, then you will get freedom from life and death. Which one is it?

Under the sea the running mud cow eats the moon.

In front of the rock, the stone tiger sleeps,
Holding a baby in his arms.

The steel snake drills into the eye of a diamond.

Mount Kun-Lun rides on the back of an elephant
Pulled by a little bird."

Can you find it? Then you will find your body, your arms, and your legs.

Yours in the Dharma,
S. S.

February 4, 1977

Dear Soen Sa Nim,

Respectfully,
Merrie

February 23, 1977

Dear Merrie,

Do you understand this? What is this?

Yours in the Dharma,
S. S.

March 12, 1977

Dear Soen Sa Nim,

Respectfully,
Merrie

March 17, 1977

Dear Merrie,

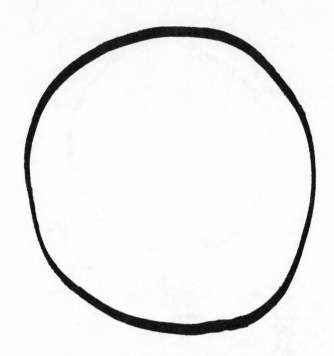

Your answer is wonderful. But you are a monkey.
Again I ask you, *what is this?*

Yours in the Dharma,
S. S.

Dear Soen Sa Nim,

Sorry to be late answering.

Respectfully,
Merrie

April 12, 1977

Dear Merrie,

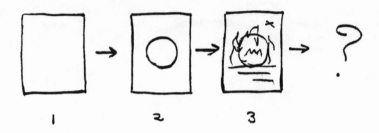

Yours in the Dharma,
S. S.

Dear Soen Sa Nim,

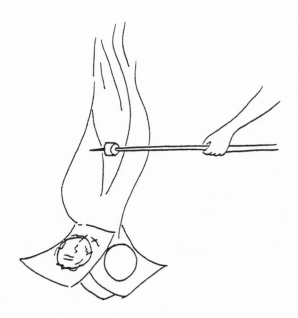

Respectfully,
Merrie

April 26, 1977

Dear Merrie,

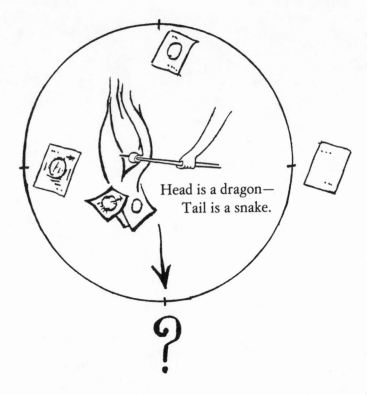

Head is a dragon—
Tail is a snake.

One more step is necessary!

Yours in the Dharma,
S. S.

May 10, 1977

Dear Soen Sa Nim,

I am in Arizona visiting my parents, but after May 17, I will be in Washington.

Have a good trip.

Respectfully,
Merrie

June 5, 1977

Dear Merrie,

Thank you for your letter. How are you?
I want a picture answer.

Yours in the Dharma,
S. S.

August 25, 1977

Dear Soen Sa Nim,

Respectfully,
Merrie

September 16, 1977

Dear Merrie,

Your answer is not bad, very good, but this is 350°, not 360°. What is "form is form; emptiness is emptiness"?

I will give you a hint. The Temple Rules [Appendix II] say, "The Great Round Mirror has no likes or dislikes."

Yours in the Dharma,
S. S.

November 6, 1977

Dear Soen Sa Nim,

Clouds come, . . . clouds. Airplane comes, . . . airplane.

Respectfully,
Merrie

November 7, 1977

Dear Merrie,

How wonderful your answer is! Wonderful, wonderful—very wonderful!

Now you understand just-like-this. Understanding just-like-this is very easy; keeping just-like-this is very difficult.

I hope you always keep just-like-this, soon finish the great work of life and death, and save all beings from suffering.

Yours in the Dharma,
S. S.

APPENDICES

APPENDIX I. "MIND MEAL"

First Gate: Jo Ju's Dog

A monk once asked Jo Ju, "Does a dog have Buddha-nature?"

Jo Ju answered, "Mu!"

1. Buddha said everything has Buddha-nature. Jo Ju said a dog has no Buddha-nature. Which one is correct?
2. Jo Ju said, "Mu!" What does this mean?
3. I ask you, does a dog have Buddha-nature?

Second Gate: Jo Ju's Washing the Bowls

A monk once asked Jo Ju, "I have just entered the monastery. Please teach me, Master."

Jo Ju said, "Have you had breakfast?"

"Yes, I have," replied the monk.

"Then," said Jo Ju, "wash your bowls."

The monk was enlightened.

What did the monk attain?

Third Gate: Seong Am Calls Master

Master Seong Am Eon used to call to himself every day, "Master!" and would answer, "Yes?"

"You must keep clear!"

"Yes!"

"Never be deceived by others, any day, any time!"

"Yes! Yes!"

Seong Am Eon used to call himself, and answer himself, two minds. Which one is the correct Master?

Fourth Gate: Bodhidharma Has No Beard

Master Hok Am said, "Why does Bodhidharma have no beard?"

1. What is Bodhidharma's original face?
2. I ask you, why does Bodhidharma have no beard?

Fifth Gate: Hyang Eom's Up A Tree

Master Hyang Eom said, "It is like a man up a tree who is hanging from a branch by his teeth; his hands cannot grasp a bough, his feet cannot touch the tree; he is tied and bound. Another man under the tree asks him, 'Why did Bodhidharma come to China?' If he does not answer, he evades his duty and will be killed. If he answers, he will lose his life. If you are in the tree, how do you stay alive?"

Sixth Gate: Dropping Ashes on the Buddha

Somebody comes to the Zen Center, smoking a cigarette. He blows smoke and drops ashes on the Buddha. If you are standing there at that time, what can you do?

Seventh Gate: Ko Bong's Three Gates

1. The sun in the sky shines everywhere. Why does a cloud obscure it?
2. Everyone has a shadow following them. How can you not step on your shadow?
3. The whole universe is on fire. Through what kind of samadhi can you escape being burned?

Eighth Gate: Duk Sahn Carrying his Bowls

One day Duk Sahn came into the Dharma Room carrying his bowls. Seol Bong (Housemaster) said, "Old Master, the bell has not yet been rung and the drum has not yet been struck. Where are you going, carrying your bowls?"

Duk Sahn returned to the Master's room. Seol Bong told Am Du (Head Monk). Am Du said, "Great Master Duk Sahn does not understand the last word."

Duk Sahn heard this and sent for Am Du. "Do you not approve of me?" he demanded. Then Am Du whispered in the Master's ear. Duk Sahn was relieved.

Next day on the rostrum, making his Dharma Speech, Duk Sahn was really different from before. Am Du went to the front of the Dharma Room, laughed loudly, clapped his hands and said, "Great joy! The old Master has understood the last word! From now on, no one can check him."

1. What was the last word?
2. What did Am Du whisper in the Master's ear?
3. How was the Master's speech different from before?

Ninth Gate: Nam Cheon Kills a Cat

Once the monks of the Eastern and Western halls were fighting about a cat. Master Nam Cheon, holding up the cat, said, "You! Give me one word and I will save this cat! If you cannot, I will kill it!" No one could answer. Finally, Nam Cheon killed the cat. In the evening, when Jo Ju returned from outside, Nam Cheon told him of the incident. Jo Ju took off his shoe, put it on his head, and walked away. Nam Cheon said, "If you had been there, I could have saved the cat."

1. Nam Cheon said, "Give me one word!" At that time, what can you do?
2. Jo Jo put his shoe on his head. What does this mean?

Tenth Gate

The mouse eats cat food, but the cat bowl is broken. What does this mean?

•

Don't make anything. Then you will get everything.
If you don't understand, only go straight—don't know.

APPENDIX II.   TEMPLE RULES

1. *On Keeping the Bodhi Mind*

You must first make a firm decision to attain Enlightenment and help others. You already have the five or the ten precepts. Know when to keep them and when to break them, when they are open and when they are closed. Let go of your small self and become your true self.

> In original nature
> There is no this and that.
> The Great Round Mirror
> Has no likes or dislikes.

2. *On Mindfulness*

Do not cling to your opinions. Do not discuss your private views with others. To cling to and defend your opinions is to destroy your practice. Put away all your opinions. This is true Buddhism.

Do not go where you have no business. Do not listen to talk which does not concern you.

Do not make the bad karma of desire, anger, or ignorance.

> If in this lifetime
> You do not open your mind,
> You cannot digest
> Even one drop of water.

3. *On Conduct*

Always act with others. Do not put yourself above others by acting differently. Arrogance is not permitted in the temple.

Money and sex are like a spiteful snake. Put your concern with them far away.

In the Dharma Room always walk behind those seated in meditation. At talks and ceremonies, keep the proper posture and dress. Do not talk or laugh loudly in the Dharma Room.

If you have business outside the temple which causes you to miss ceremonies or meals, notify one of the temple officials before you leave.

Respect those older than you. Love those younger than you. Keep your mind large and open.

If you meet sick people, love and help them.

Be hospitable to guests. Make them welcome and attend to their needs.

When respected people visit the temple, bow to them and speak considerately to them.

Be courteous. Always let others go before you.

Help other people.

Do not play games with other people.

Do not gossip.

Do not use other people's shoes and coats.

Do not cling to the scriptures.

Do not oversleep.

Do not be frivolous.

Let older and more respected people be seated before you.

Do not discuss petty temple matters with guests.

When visiting outside the temple, speak well of the temple to others.

Drinking to produce heedlessness, or acting out of lust, will only make bad karma and destroy your practice. You must be strong and think correctly. Then these desires cannot tempt you.

Do not delude yourself into thinking you are a great and free person. This is not true Buddhism.

Attend only to yourself. Do not judge the actions of others.

Do not make the bad karma of killing, stealing, or of lust.

Originally there is nothing.
But Buddha practiced unmoving under the
    Bodhi tree for six years.
And for nine years Bodhidharma sat
    silently in Sorim.

If you can break the wall of your self,
You will become infinite in time and space.

4. *On Speech*

Your evil tongue will lead you to ruin. You must keep the stopper in the bottle. Only open it when necessary.

Always speak well, in the manner of a Bodhisattva. Do not use vulgar language in the temple.

If you come upon two people fighting, do not provoke them by angry speech. Rather use good words to soothe their anger.

Do not make the bad karma of lying, exaggerating, making trouble between people, or cursing others.

Once a man spoke incorrectly and was reborn
    a fox for 500 generations. After he heard
    the correct speech, he lost his fox's body.

What is correct and incorrect speech?

If you open your mouth, I will hit you thirty times.
If you close your mouth, I will still hit you thirty times.

You must grab the word-head (kong-an) and not let go.

The dog is barking. Wong, wong, wong!

The cat is meowing. Meow, meow, meow.

5. *On Eating*

An eminent teacher said, "A day without work is a day without eating."

There are two kinds of work: inside work and outside work. Inside work is keeping clear mind. Outside work is cutting off selfish desires and helping others.

First work, then eat.

Eat in silence. Do not make unnecessary noise.

While eating, attend only to yourself. Do not be concerned with the actions of others.

Accept what is served with gratitude. Do not cling to your likes and dislikes.

Do not seek satisfaction in eating. Eat only to support yourself in your practice.

Though you may eat good food all your life, your body will die.

> The Great Way is not difficult.
> Simply cut off all thought of good and bad.

> Salt is salty.
> Sugar is sweet.

6. *On Formal Practice*

During formal practice act with other people.

Do not be lazy.

During chanting, follow the moktak.

During sitting, follow the chugpi.

Perceive the true meaning of chanting and sitting and act accordingly.

Understand that you have accumulated bad karma which is like a big mountain. Keep this in mind as you bow in repentance.

Our karma has no self-nature, but is created by our mind. If our mind is extinguished, our karma will be extinguished. When we see both as empty, this is true repentance. We bow to see true nature and help others.

Shouting into a valley.
Big shout: big echo.
Small shout: small echo.

7. *On the Dharma Talk*

When you listen to the words of the Zen Master, keep your mind clear. Do not be attached to his words. Cut off all thought and pierce the true meaning of his speech.

Do not think, "I already have great understanding; I have no use for this speech." This is delusion.

If you have a question, put it to the Zen Master after he is finished speaking.

If a snake drinks water, the water becomes venom. If a cow drinks water, the water becomes milk. If you cling to ignorance, you create life and death. If you keep clear, you become Buddha.

In the great work of life and death,
    time will not wait for you.
If you die tomorrow, what kind of body will you get?
Is not all of this of great importance?

Hurry up! Hurry!

Blue sky and green sea
Are the Buddha's original face.

The sound of the waterfall and the bird's song
Are the great sutras.

Where are you going?
Watch your step.

Water flows down to the sea.
Clouds float up to the heavens.

APPENDIX III.   THE HEART SUTRA

The Maha Prajna Paramita Hrdaya Sutra

Avalokitesvara Bodhisattva when practicing deeply the Prajna Paramita perceives that all five skandhas are empty and is saved from all suffering and distress.

Shariputra, form does not differ from emptiness, emptiness does not differ from form. That which is form is emptiness, that which is emptiness form. The same is true of feelings, perceptions, impulses, consciousness.

Shariputra, all dharmas are marked with emptiness. They do not appear or disappear, are not tainted or pure, do not increase or decrease. Therefore in emptiness no form, no feelings, perceptions, impulses, consciousness. No eyes, no ears, no nose, no tongue, no body, no mind, no color, no sound, no smell, no taste, no touch, no object of mind, no realm of eyes, and so forth until no realm of mind consciousness. No ignorance and also no extinction of it, and so forth until no old age and death and also no extinction of them. No suffering, no origination, no stopping, no path, no cognition, also no attainment with nothing to attain.

The Bodhisattva depends on Prajna Paramita and the mind is no hindrance; without any hindrance no fears exist. Far apart from every perverted view one dwells in Nirvana.

In the three worlds all Buddhas depend on Prajna Paramita and attain Anuttara Samyak Sambodhi.

Therefore know that Prajna Paramita is the great transcendent mantra, is the great bright mantra, is the utmost mantra, is the supreme mantra which is able to relieve all suffering and is true, not false. So proclaim the Prajna Paramita mantra, proclaim the mantra which says:

gate gate paragate parasamgate bodhi svaha
gate gate paragate parasamgate bodhi svaha
gate gate paragate parasamgate bodhi svaha

APPENDIX IV.   THE FIVE PRECEPTS

I vow to abstain from taking life.

I vow to abstain from taking things not given.

I vow to abstain from misconduct done in lust.

I vow to abstain from lying.

I vow to abstain from intoxicants,
   taken to induce heedlessness.

APPENDIX V: THE ZEN CIRCLE

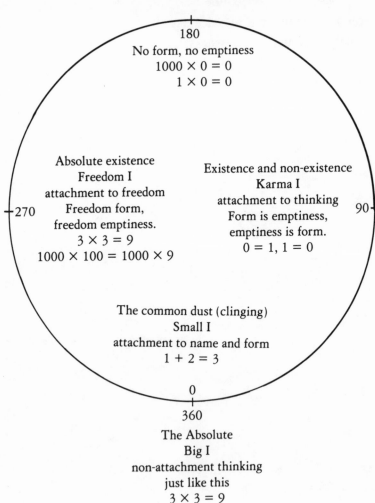

True emptiness
Nothing I
attachment to emptiness

180
No form, no emptiness
$1000 \times 0 = 0$
$1 \times 0 = 0$

Absolute existence
Freedom I
attachment to freedom
Freedom form,
freedom emptiness.
$3 \times 3 = 9$
$1000 \times 100 = 1000 \times 9$

270

Existence and non-existence
Karma I
attachment to thinking
Form is emptiness,
emptiness is form.
$0 = 1, 1 = 0$

90

The common dust (clinging)
Small I
attachment to name and form
$1 + 2 = 3$

0
360
The Absolute
Big I
non-attachment thinking
just like this
$3 \times 3 = 9$

Form is form, emptiness is emptiness.

APPENDIX VI.   GLOSSARY

Beads: A string of beads resembling a bracelet or necklace, used for counting bows or repetitions of a mantra in various sects of Buddhism. Similar to a rosary.

Bodhisattva (Sanskrit): *Bodhi* means perfect wisdom or prajna, and *sattva* means a being whose actions promote unity or harmony. One who vows to postpone the still bliss of Enlightenment in order to help all sentient beings realize their own liberation; one who seeks Enlightenment not only for himself but for others. The Bodhisattva ideal is at the heart of Mahayana and Zen Buddhism.

Buddha-nature: That which all sentient beings share and manifest through their particular form. According to the Zen school of Buddhism, the Buddha said that all things have Buddha-nature and therefore have the innate potential to become Buddha.

Compass of Zen Teaching: A handbook compiled by Zen Master Seung Sahn containing an outline of the basic teachings of Buddhism in the Theravada, Mahayana, and Zen traditions. The *Compass* includes several additional selections: "Mind Meal," Temple Rules, the Chogye lineage of patriarchs from the Buddha to the present, and the Ten Great Vows.

Dharma Room: In Zen Master Seung Sahn's Zen Centers it is the meditation and ceremony hall.

Dharma Teacher: An older student who takes an additional Five Precepts and accepts the responsibility to teach new students about Zen practice.

Five Precepts: Appendix IV.

Four Bowls: The bowls used during formal meals in Zen Centers under Zen Master Seung Sahn's direction. Formal meals eaten in silence are a traditional part of Zen practice. Each person takes the quantity of food he wants and then cleans his bowls with tea and water so that no trace of food remains.

Hapchang (Korean), [Gasshō (Japanese)]: The gesture of placing the hands palm to palm before the chest to indicate respect, gratitude, and humility.

Hara (Japanese): The vital energy center of the abdomen; in many Zen traditions it is considered to be the seat of the heart-body-mind. Focusing one's attention on the hara is a technique used in some forms of Zen practice for centering and developing samadhi power.

Heart Sutra: Appendix III.

Interview: A formal, private meeting between a Zen teacher and a student in which kong-ans are used to test and stimulate the student's practice; may also occasion informal questions and instruction.

Kalpa (Sanskrit): An eon; the time period during which the physical universe is formed and destroyed. An unimaginably long period of time.

Karma (Sanskrit): Karma means "cause and effect," and the continuing process of action and reaction, accounting for the interpenetration of all phenomena. Thus our present thoughts, actions, and situations are the result of what we have done in the past, and our future thoughts, actions, and situations will be the product of what we are doing now. All individual karma results from this process.

Kayagum (Korean): A stringed musical instrument of Korean origin.

Kido (Korean): Literally, "energy way"; a chanting retreat.

Kong-an (Korean) [Kung-an (Chinese), Koan (Japanese)]: Literally, "a public notice issued by the government." In Zen practice, kong-ans are the recorded sayings, actions, or dialogues of Zen Masters with their students or with other Zen Masters. They are the core of Zen teaching literature. As a tool in practice, they are used by a Zen Master to test the intuitive clarity of a student's mind, or to bring a student from thinking back to "don't-know." There are approximately 1,700 traditional kong-ans.

Kong-an Book: The collection of letters written to Zen Master Seung Sahn and his replies. It also includes poems and short talks by him and talks and correspondence by Master Dharma Teachers George Bowman and Barbara Rhodes. Selections from the kong-an book are read each morning and evening at Zen Centers under Zen Master Seung Sahn's direction.

Kwan Seum Bosal (Korean); [Avalokitesvara (Sanskrit); Kwan (Shih) Yin (Chinese); Kwan Um (Korean); Kannon, Kanzaon (Japanese)]: Literally, "One who perceives the Cries of the World" and responds with compassionate aid, the Bodhisattva of compassion.

Mantra (Sanskrit): Sounds or words used in Zen practice in the Korean tradition to cut through discriminating thought so that the mind can become clear; in some practices, mantra is used to induce various kinds of insight.

Master Dharma Teacher: A student who has been authorized by Zen Master Seung Sahn to teach kong-an practice and run meditation retreats because of the strength of his or her practice.

"Mind Meal": Appendix I.

Moktak (Korean): A gourd-like instrument used to set the rhythm during chanting.

Roshi (Japanese): "Venerable (spiritual) teacher," a Zen Master.

Samadhi (Sanskrit): A state of intense concentration.

Samsara (Sanskrit): Transmigration. Originally it meant "flow" as in the continuous cycle of birth and death; the endless transformation of all phenomena in accordance with the law of causation, or karma.

Sangha (Sanskrit): In the Theravada tradition, an assembly or brotherhood of monks. In the Mahayana and Zen traditions, the community of all Buddhists. May refer to a family of students under a particular master.

Sanjo (Korean): A stringed instrument similar to a guitar.

Satori (Japanese): The experience of awakening. Enlightenment.

Soen Sa Nim (Korean): "Honored Zen teacher," a Zen Master.

Temple Rules: Appendix II.

Yong Maeng Jong Jin (Korean): Literally, "valorous or intrepid concentration," sometimes paraphrased, "to leap like a tiger while sitting." In the West it is a two-, three-, or seven-day silent retreat involving thirteen hours of formal meditation practice a day. Participants follow a schedule of bowing, sitting, chanting, eating, and working, with an emphasis on sitting meditation. During the retreat each participant has interviews with the Zen Master or a Master Dharma Teacher.

Zen Center(s): Meditation communities, some of which include a residence. All the Zen Centers in the Kwan Um School of Zen are under the spiritual direction of Zen Master Seung Sahn, and each offers regular practice and periodic retreats.

Primary Point Press is the publications division of the Kwan Um School of Zen. It has also published *Gathering of Spirit: Women Teaching in American Buddhism*, edited by Ellen S. Sidor (1987; third edition 1992); *Ten Gates: The Kong-an Teaching of Zen Master Seung Sahn* (1987); *Thousand Peaks: Korean Zen — Traditions and Teachers*, by Mu Soeng Sunim (second edition 1991); and *Heart Sutra: Ancient Buddhist Wisdom in the Light of Quantum Reality*, by Mu Soeng Sunim (1991).

The Kwan Um School of Zen is a network of centers under the spiritual direction of Zen Master Seung Sahn and senior teachers. The school publishes *Primary Point,* an international journal of Buddhism. More information about the Kwan Um School of Zen, including a list of centers worldwide, may be received by contacting the school at:

528 Pound Road, Cumberland, Rhode Island 02864
Telephone (401) 658-1476   FAX (401) 658-1188